Harald Jes

Lizards in the Terrarium

Buying, Feeding, Care, Sicknesses,
with a Special Chapter on Setting Up
Rain-Forest, Desert, and Water Terrariums.

With Color Photographs by Well-Known Photographers
and Drawings by Fritz W. Kohler

Translated from the German
by Elizabeth D. Crawford

American Consulting Editor
Fredrik L. Frye DVM, MS
Clinical Professor of Medicine
School of Veterinary Medicine
University of California, Davis

BARRON'S

English translation ©Copyright 1987
by Barron's Educational Series, Inc.

© Copyright 1987 by Grafe and Unzer
GmbH, Munich, West Germany

The Title of the German book is *Echsen als
Terrarientiere*

All inquiries should be addressed to:
Barron's Educational Series, Inc.
250 Wireless Boulevard
Hauppauge, NY 11788

International Standard Book No. 0-8120-3925-4
Library of Congress Catalog Card No. 87-26911

Library of Congress Cataloging-in-Publication Data

Jes, Harald.
    Lizards in the terrarium.

    Translation of: Echsen als Terrarientiere.
    Bibliography: p.
    Includes index.
    1. Lizards as pets.   2. Terrariums.   I. Title.
SF459.L5J4713   1987   639.3'95   87-26911
ISBN 0-8120-3925-4

Printed and Bound in China

3   490   13 12

The color photos on the cover show

Front cover: Soa-soa *(Hydrosaurus amboinensis)*
Inside/front cover: double-crested basilisk *(Basiliscus
plunifrons),* male: Freiland-photograph. Inside back
cover: tame common iguana *(Iguana iguana).* Back
cover: Top left, Tokay gecko *(Gecko gecko);* top right,
dwarf caiman *(Paleosuchus palpebrosus);* bottom left,
common iguana *(Iguana iguana);* bottom right,
Madagascar gecko *(Phelsuma laricauda)*

Note and Warning

This book describes electrical equipment for use in the
care of lizards and terrariums. *Important:* Read the
section of "Avoiding Electrical Accidents" on page
15; otherwise very serious accidents can occur.
While handling lizards you can receive bite wounds,
tail blows, or scratches. Even the smallest scratch
requires immediate medical attention—only a doctor
can provide the right treatment (see page 62).
Be especially careful that children do not eat
terrarium plants. These can cause serious injuries.
Some of the plants described have juices that
produce dangerous reactions if they come in contact
with the skin or mucous membranes of
human beings.
In addition, animals can become infected with sicknesses that are transferrable to humans. After
working in the terrarium with plants or animals,
wash your hands thoroughly; any splashes that have
reached your face should be flushed away
immediately.

Photo Credits

Angermayer: page 10, back cover (bottom left); Angermayer/
Reinhard: page 54 (top right); Cramm: page 35 (top) 36 (top left;
middle left); Dossenback: page 53 (middle left); Kahl: page 53
(top left; top right) 63 (top left), 64 (bottom left), back cover (top
left; bottom right); Koch: page 9, (top, bottom); Konig: page 53,
(bottom left; bottom right), 64 (top left), back cover, (top right);
Meier: page 36 (bottom left), 54 (bottom); Meyer: page 64
(middle right), Muller: front cover; Podloucky: page 63
(bottom); Reinhard: page 35 (bottom right) 36 (middle right), 63
(top right); Trutnau: page 35 (bottom left), 36 (bottom right), 64
(top right; middle left; bottom right); Walther: back cover
(inside); Wothe: front cover (inside); Ziehm: page 36 (top right),
53 (middle right); Ziesler: page 54 (top left)

About the Author

Harald Jes is the director of the Aquarium am Zoo
in Cologne, West Germany, and has played a crucial
role in its creation and developement. He has been
involved with the care of reptiles for almost 40 years.
His special interest lies in lizard breeding; under his
direction the Cologne Zoo has succeeded in breeding
dwarf caiman in the terrarium for the first time.

Contents

Preface

Learning To Understand Lizards 5
Some Information About Lizards 5
Important Behavior Patterns 8

The Right Terrarium 12
The Terrarium 12
The Sun Terrarium 13

Terrarium Technology 15
Avoiding Electrical Accidents 15
Heating 15
Lighting 16
Ultraviolet Light 17
Regulation of Temperature and Light 17
Maintaining Water Purity 18

Rain-Forest, Desert, And Water Terrariums
The Rain-Forest Terrarium 19
The Desert Terrarium 20
The Water Terrarium 22

Purchase and Quarantine 24
Endangered Species Regulations 24
Where You Buy Lizards 24
Advice on Buying Lizards 24
Carrying Your Lizard Home 25
Settling In 25

Feeding 27
Plant Food 27
Animal Food 27
Vitamins 28
Minerals 28
Proper Feeding 29
Force-Feeding 30

Keeping And Breeding Food Animals 31
Insects 31
Small Mammals 33

Basic Care And Maintenance 34
Important Rules for the Lizard-Keeper 34
Controlling the Climate in the Terrarium 34
Cleaning the Terrarium 37

Body Care Procedures 38
Holding Lizards Properly 38
Avoiding Stress Situations in the Terrarium 39
Care of Your Lizards When You Go
     on Vacation 40

Introduction to Lizard Breeding 41
The Parent Animals 41
Prerequisites for Mating 42
Courtship 42
Mating 42
Egg-Laying 43
Transferring the Eggs to the Incubator 43
The Young Animal 44
Live-bearing Lizards 45

Sickness 46
Illnesses Diagnosed with the Naked Eye 46
Sicknesses and Parasites Diagnosed by Fecal
     Examination or Section 51

Plant In The Terrarium 56
Location of the Planted Terrarium 56
Planting Medium 56
Watering 57
Plant Pests 57
Changing Plants 57
Choosing the Plants 57
Plants from North, South, and Central America 58
Plants from Southeast Asia 59
Plants from Africa 60
Plants from Australia 61
Plants from the Islands of the Western
     Mediterranean 61

**Setting Up Desert, Rain-Forest, And Water
Terrariums** 62
Description of the species with information about
behavior, size of terrarium, and fittings, as well as
care and feeding.

Books for Further Help 85

Index 86

Preface

Keeping lizards is a hobby that is fascinating and fun, but it is also a responsible undertaking, demanding expert knowledge, capacity for understanding, and the power of observation. These cold-blooded animals, which often look like miniature editions of prehistoric saurians, are much less adaptable than warm-blooded house pets like birds, small mammals, dogs, and cats. Therefore lizards can only be maintained in the terrarium successfully when their requirements for living space, climate, and food can be met.

Harald Jes, who as a zoo expert has special experience in keeping and breeding lizards, tells what is necessary for keeping lizards in a terrarium. He gives advice on how to buy the right terrarium and how to ventilate, heat, and light it, in terms so easily understood that even a beginner can follow them. Rule number one is that the lizard-keeper must know as much as possible about the life needs of the animals. Today lizards that can be kept in a terrarium come from a wide variety of the environments of our earth — from dry desert regions to tropical rain forests. The various requirements that result for the keeping and care of lizards are described in detail in the special chapter on the arrangement of desert, rain-forest, and semiaquatic terraria. The lizard-keeper can thus determine easily what is necessary for the appropriate care of the particular lizards he has chosen.

Proper feeding is very important for the proper maintenance of lizards and takes on a special significance at the time the animals are obtained. The keeper of a lizard that requires animal food will have little pleasure if he finds it difficult to kill animals for food.

It would be wiser to choose an herbivorous lizard. The chapter on feeding gives exact information about the appropriate food and the proper method of feeding for both carnivorous and herbivorous lizards. Information about keeping and breeding food animals is given on page 31.

Without doubt the most fascinating thing about keeping lizards is observing the many patterns of typical behavior that each species displays in the appropriate environment. The better suited the terrarium environment is to the particular requirements of the lizards, the more likely that they will mate and that the offspring can be raised.

A word needs to be said about the protection of endangered species. If you take on the responsibility for lizards you must realize that you cannot just pick out any you might like. For one thing, there are certain lizard species that definitely cannot be kept in a terrarium — or can be maintained only under the most difficult conditions, nearly impossible for a layperson to fulfill; for another, there are national and international endangered-species agreements that govern the purchase or possession of some lizards. These restrictions are listed on pages 24 to 62 and are discussed in detail.

Author and publisher thank everyone who has made possible the illustration of this book with strikingly beautiful color photographs and informative drawings: the animal artist Fritz W. Kohler and the animal photographers listed on the copyright page of this book. Thanks, too, to the Cologne Aquarium and Zoo and to the Darmstadt Vivarium for permission to take the lizard photographs for this book.

Learning to Understand Lizards

Some Information About Lizards

Lizards, which belong to the class Reptilia, resemble the dragons of the old fairy tales and the gigantic dinosaurs of long-ago eras. With their scaly skin, their mostly immovable eyes, and a circulatory system that does not provide the body with warmth, they have long been less familiar to us than mammals or birds. Anyone who wants to keep lizards in a terrarium should know at the start what these animals are like and where they come from. Lizards' body structure, behavior, and living habits provide the lizard-keeper with very important indications for their care and maintenance.

Origins

Fossil finds provide evidence that the first lizards lived on the earth some 260 million years ago — in the Upper Carboniferous Period. But because even by this time they already existed in many forms, it is clear that there had been a common ancestor earlier. Only the turtles and the Rhynchocephalian tuatara persist into our time. Some 120 million years ago the crocodilians arose. The present-day lizards today number some 3,000 species. They are spread throughout the temperate zones of the earth, thought most species live in the tropical zones.

Limbs

The limbs of the lizard give an indication of its way of life:

Tree-dwelling, fast-climbing species have long, delicately jointed legs — especially the tibia (shinbone). These lizards have extremely long feet and long toes, which are armed with sharp claws. There may also be fringes of skin on the toes that enable the lizard to run on its two hind legs across a flooded area (see drawing below).

Terrestrial lizards have short, powerful extremities and heavy feet. Many of them can dig holes and tunnels in the earth.

Water-dwelling lizards have short, powerful limbs and as an adaptation for the aquatic life style they have webs between the toes; these vary in nature from species to species. Many semiaquatic lizards use their flattened tails to help propel them through the water.

Special adaptations are the gripping lamellae (platelike growths) on the undersides of the toes of most geckos (see drawing on page 39). On the lamellae are microscopic hooked cells, which enable the geckos to maintain a grip on smooth surfaces such as large leaves, ceilings, and even on glass.

The common basilisk can run across the water quickly using only its hind legs.

Tail

Some species of lizards can, in reaction to an extreme stimulus, cast off the tail or a

Learning to Understand Lizards

portion of the tail. This behavior, which is called autotomy, is an important defense mechanism. A predator is easily distracted by the cast-off tail, all the more as the tail segment may continue to make slithering movements for a while because it possesses an independent nervous system. Lizards that autotomize have tail vertebrae with pre-established breaking points. The shortened tail regenerates partly or wholly, not by means of new bony tail vertebrae but by developing new cartilage. The appearance of the scales and the color may not always match those of the lost tail.

Sensory organs

The eyes: Probably the most important sense organs for the lizard are the eyes. In most lizards, the sense of sight is very well developed, even allowing them to perceive colors. Evidence for this comes principally from the many optical signals through which lizards identify each other or communicate (see Important Behavior Patterns, page 8).

In species active at night or at dusk, the pupils are slit-shaped, to protect the eye from glaring light. As light dims, the slit widens.

At the base of the eyelid are the tear glands; on the nictitating membrane (a third, often translucent eyelid) are the lachrymal and Harderian glands. (Iguanas excrete salt through specialized "salt glands" that are located in their nasal cavities. This salt is sneezed out. Thus many a sneezing iguana is not an iguana with a cold.)

The ears: Hearing abilities vary greatly from species to species. Unlike the lizards, the crocodilians have an external auditory canal (see Dwarf caiman, page 62). Some hear well and are even able to distinguish specific noises. For example, geckos have comparatively good hearing; the sounds and cries that they emit during mating, particularly, are an indication of this.

The tongue: Aromatic substances are taken onto the tongue tip when the tongue is extended and are deposited into the roof of the mouth where the Jacobson's organ is located. The perception of the aromatic substance is accomplished through the sensory-cell tissue of this organ. Therefore, increased darting of the tongue — at feeding, for example — is analogous to the excited sniffing of a dog.

After eating, many lizards polish their mouth with their tongue. Almost all use it to drink or — to put it more accurately — to flick up the water. Geckos that lack movable eyelids regularly polish their eyes with their fleshy tongues. Lizards' tongues differ from species to species. They can be deeply cleft and extended, serpentlike (see drawing below). By means of a notch in the upper jaw, the monitor lizard, for instance, can flick its tongue with its jaws closed. But tongues can also be short and fleshy, as in the iguana.

Komodo dragon with darting tongue. The monitor has a notch in the upper jaw that allows its tongue to dart when the jaws are closed.

Learning to Understand Lizards

Skin

In most lizards the skin is very highly developed. It consists of scales and sometimes bony plates of different sizes and shapes, whose arrangement is always the same within each species but differs within the orders, families, and genera. In the zoological classification of lizards, therefore, the scales serve for recognition and definition. Since the lizard skin is horny on the surface — the surface a lifeless structure that no longer grows — it does not continue to fit during the period when the lizard is still growing. Therefore the skin must be shed from time to time. The lizard molts. The new skin is somewhat larger than the old. The fast-growing young lizard molts at substantially shorter intervals than the more slowly growing older animal, but even mature lizards shed their epidermal skin surface as it becomes worn.

Molting is governed by the hormones of the pituitary and thyroid glands, although external factors like temperature, humidity, food supply, and the condition of the animal in general also play a role. The molting proceeds differently among the various kinds of lizards:

Skinks slip out of their skin like snakes and leave it behind all in one piece.

Other lizards, like the monitors, lose their skin in patches or shreds. This often continues for so long that an entirely new molting is beginning at the head as the skin on the tail is just sloughing off.

Geckos grasp the old skin in their mouth, pull it from the body, and eat it, thereby taking in valuable nutrients.

The changing color of the skin is brought about by the expansion and contraction of the pigment in the color cells of the dermis and lower epidermis. The color change is controlled by hormones or by the nervous system. It can be an adaptation to the background or, frequently, it is a reaction to the mood of the lizard. Threats, displaying, courtship, or mating can influence the color range of many lizard species. Dark colors mostly signify rest or submission, but they will also appear when it is important for the lizard to take up as much solar energy as possible.

Leopard gecko after molting. The gecko consumes the old skin and thus takes in valuable nutrients.

Body temperature

Reptiles, including the lizards, are described as cold-blooded or poikilothermic animals. This means that their body temperature is influenced by the temperature of their surroundings, since — in contrast to mammals and birds — they do not possess (or do so to only a very marginal degree) the power of keeping their body temperature constant. The body temperature can be higher than the environmental temperature when a sunbath-

Learning to Understand Lizards

ing lizard has become dark and is thereby taking up much warmth from the sun. It can be less if a bright color is reflecting the sun. If the heat of the sun becomes too great, lizards seek shadow or damp places in the earth.

Since the blood distributes warmth throughout the body, it follows that the heartbeat can exercise a degree of influence over the body temperature.

Hints for care: Because lizards cannot accommodate themselves to extreme variations of climate, the lizard-keeper must see to it that the temperature in the terrarium corresponds to the needs of the captive lizard species. You will find exact temperature requirements in the descriptions of particular lizards, which begins on page 62.

Important Behavior Patterns

Some particularly striking behavior patterns are easy to observe in the terrarium. For example, you can draw conclusions about the mood of the lizard or tell if the animal in the terrarium is under stress.

Threatening behavior

Threatening demeanor varies from species to species.

- Iguanas threaten a rival by stalking stiff-legged with mouth wide open and trunk vertical and flattened, head nodding, and presenting the dewlap.
- Bearded lizards threaten with wide-open mouth and prickly black beard — a fold of skin on the neck — erected. The shining yellow mucous membrane of the mouth thus contrasts strikingly with the dark beard.

- Blue-tongued skinks achieve a similarly terrifying effect with a wide-open mouth, thus exhibiting their shimmering gray-blue tongue and the red mucous membrane of their mouth.
- "True" lizards (Lacertidae) threaten by high-stepping with head thrown backward.
- Male anoles nod their heads and erect the dewlap on their necks when they are menacing another lizard (see drawing at right).
- Monitor lizards signal an attack by high-stepping with head sunk and agitated puffing up of trunk and neck.
- There are also less striking modes of behavior that permit the instant recognition of lizards' moods — for example, the leopard gecko's excited vibration of the tip of its tail that signals an impending attack.

It is important for the keeper to recognize the threatening behavior of his lizards.

Lizards threaten each other according to a typical ritual — it is a part of their method of communication — but the threat may also be directed toward the keeper. In that case, special caution is indicated. A blow from an iguana's tail or from that of a larger monitor can be painful, as can the bite of a Tokay gecko.

Sample terrariums: Top: Rain-forest terrarium with double-crested basilisk *(Basiliscus plumifrons).* Bottom: Desert terrarium with spiny tailed skink *(Egernia cunninghami).*

Learning to Understand Lizards

Important: If you are bitten by a lizard, see a doctor at once.

A lizard that is constantly being threatened by another lizard is placed under constant psychological stress. An animal so threatened will languish if the caretaker does not intervene promptly (see page 39).

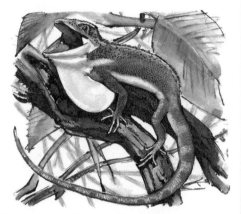

Threatening knight anole. The male anole erects the dewlap on its neck when it threatens another lizard or during courtship rituals.

Submissive behavior

A typical submissive behavior pattern is the "treading" of a submissive true lizard. Lying with head and front part of the body raised, it moves the front legs quickly up and down, while the dominant animal threatens with head held upward and legs high. When an animal shows this submissive pattern frequently, the caretaker must intervene to help by providing better territorial boundaries in the terrarium or, if necessary, putting the dominated animal in a separate terrarium (see Avoiding Stress Situations in the terrarium, page 39).

Oriental (Chinese) water dragons *(Physignathus concincinus).* Young animals, six to nine months old.

The Right Terrarium

A lizard-keeper who cares about the well-being of his animals will have the necessary sense of responsibility to provide the appropriate environment for them, for only when the living needs of the particular lizard species are met can the animals be comfortable, live a long time, and perhaps even reproduce. Neglect or skimping for the wrong reasons, either on the terrarium or the equipment, lead only to disappointment, quite apart from the bad conscience that must result if you are responsible for the illness or death of an animal.

The Terrarium

If you are buying a terrarium in a pet store, it is a matter of taste whether you choose a frame, all-glass, or wooden terrarium. Whatever you decide, be sure that the terrarium is well made and easy to clean and maintain.

If you want to build the terrarium yourself, you should have some experience with carpentry. Get advice from the pet store or hobby shop.

Size

It is impossible to give a rule for calculating the size of a terrarium. Lizards' space requirements depend not only on their size but above all on their behavior. So comparatively small species may, because of their territorial behavior, require much space. These animals establish territories and defend them. They suffer if the terrarium can't be divided into territories because it is arranged wrong or there are too many animals living in it. The size of the terrarium also depends on the number of animals you want to keep.

Obviously you must allow for freedom of movement for the particular kind of lizard. In certain cases larger lizards require markedly less space, because they are neither territorial nor free-ranging. You will find helpful information in the last chapter (see page 62) about the details of terrarium size and the suitable number of lizards.

Shape

Pet stores mostly carry the oblong, all-purpose terrariums, which are about twice as long as they are wide and just as high as they are wide (ratio 2:1:1; length:width:height). Very nearly all lizards can be accommodated in such a terrarium, and a suitable place can be found for it in any dwelling. Lizards that live in treetops, tree trunks, or in stone walls require a terrarium that is twice as high as it is wide (1:2:2). If the terrarium is free-standing with space around it and perhaps has an island of wood or stone in the middle, a cube shape would be appropriate.

Location

What shape and size terrarium you choose also depends on where you plan to put it. It can be free-standing or it can be built into a wall of shelves. If you are thinking of building one in, you must consider beforehand how the terrarium can be heated, ventilated, and lighted without problems.

Ventilation

An important prerequisite for the successful care of lizards is the provision of fresh air. Nowhere — not even in the most stifling tropical jungle — is there so little movement of air as there is in a space that is enclosed on all sides.

The Right Terrarium

Covering: A cover is necessary for most terrariums. The largest part of the terrarium roof must be of wire screen. The size of the mesh and the weight of the wire should be chosen so that neither lizards nor food animals can escape. Plastic mesh is unsuitable because the heat of the spotlights (see page 15) can melt it and the ultraviolet radiation of the therapeutic lamps (see page 17) can cause it to deteriorate.

Side-wall ventilation: One of the side walls of the terrarium must be perforated over the lower third to an area of at least 10 percent of the area of the terrarium (length x width of the terrarium floor) or be made of wire mesh. This is the only way to allow for air to combine with the influx from the heat supply to create thermal movement.

Technical aids to ventilation: If roof and side ventilation are not possible because you cannot undertake the appropriate construction changes or you want to build the terrarium in, you must use mechanical ventilation. An aquarium air pump with an air tube having an interior diameter of 0.2 inches (5 mm) is suitable for this purpose. The tube should be directed to the floor of the terrarium and fastened so that the air is expelled horizontally. You can also install a rotary or tangential fan, by means of which air is pressed or sucked into the tank through a shaft (consult with the pet store). Bear in mind that only a very small amount of air movement is required in a terrarium, so you must regulate the equipment so that you don't generate a storm. Be careful, too, that only clean, temperate air is drawn into the terrarium. Cold air or air polluted with tobacco smoke or pigment solvents will injure the lizards.

Doors

It is very helpful, especially in larger terrariums, if one of the long sides can be opened so you can work in the terrarium unhindered. A glass door that can be slid to one side or overhead is advisable. Then you can reach everywhere in the tank without having to open the whole front — which is a special advantage with fleet-footed lizards, ever poised for escape. To keep the terrarium floor material from clogging the track for the sliding doors, the track should run 4 inches (10 cm) above the bottom of the terrarium. Sand and earth will block the door (or the rollers in the case of large plates of glass), which can break the glass.

The Sun Terrarium

On sunny summer days you can bring your lizards out into the fresh air for a few hours. It does them good to enjoy sunlight that is not filtered through glass by being in a wire cage on a balcony or in a yard. You don't have to be particularly handy with tools to build a cage of lath and wire mesh yourself (see drawing below).

● It needn't be as large as the terrarium, but it should allow the lizards enough room to move around.

● The wire mesh should be fine enough and strong enough to keep the lizards from escaping.

● A bathing place for the lizards is important; it should be large enough so that there is enough room in it for the whole lizard.

● You must cover one part of the cage so that the lizards can withdraw into the shade. This is important, because the sun — even in the

The Right Terrarium

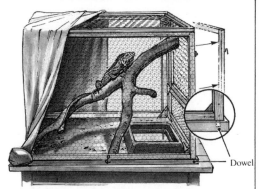

Dowel

Homemade sun terrarium with a door opening at the side. It is important to have a water bath and a shady corner. The detailed drawing shows how frame pieces and floor are securely jointed by means of a dowel.

northern latitudes — can exceed the temperature ranges that are tolerable for reptiles, and the lizards, at least during the early summer, are not yet used to the effects of direct sunlight.

The lizards can also stay in their own terrarium for their sunbath if you put it on a wheeled base and roll it outside. A shady corner is particularly necessary in this case, and above all you must keep very careful watch on the temperature in the terrarium. In a cage that is mostly glassed in, the danger of overheating is very great!

Terrarium Technology

To create a suitable living space for lizards you must use equipment such as heaters, filters, lamps, and the ventilation equipment already described on page 13.

Avoiding Electrical Accidents

You must use caution when dealing with electrical equipment and wiring, which are especially dangerous when used in connection with water. The following precautions should be carefully observed at all times:

• The electrical equipment described in this book must carry the UL symbol.

• All lamps used must be isolated from water or spray.

• Equipment that will be operated in the water portion of a terrarium must carry the notice that it is suitable for underwater use.

• Pull the main plug before you do any work in a water terrarium or remove any equipment. This will not only ensure your own safety but will also avoid injury to the heater (see page 16).

• If your electric current does not already pass through a central fuse box or circuit-breaker, it is advisable to install a suitable fuse in each switch box. The fuse will interrupt the flow of current as soon as there is any failure in the equipment or wiring. You can buy variable fuses or circuit-breakers or other power-failure safety controls in an electrical-supply or hardware store. A central fuse box or circuit-breaker system can only be installed by a licensed electrician!

Heating

Reflector lamps

Many lizards associate the warmth that is so necessary for them with light; they do not respond to warmth by itself. Therefore they need a heat source that gives light at the same time. For these animals you can install incandescent lamps. They are sold in stores as reflector spotlights. The wattage and the potential surface temperature you need depend on the requirements of the particular type of lizard (temperature requirements are given in the chapter on Setting Up Terrariums, page 62). Spotlights are available in wattages of 25 to 150 and with a beam angle of 30 to 80 degrees, so the right spotlight is available for every size terrarium and for every possible construction. Wherever there is splashing water to contend with, you must use a safety-glass reflector lamp. The thin-walled glass reflector lamps will not survive water splashes.

Infrared lamps

For the less light-dependent lizards, such as geckos, infrared lamps (60 to 250 watts) can be installed for heat sources. They don't burn out as fast as spotlights and are therefore cheaper in the long run.

Installing the heat supply: Spotlights and heat lamps must be installed in such a way that the lizards can't reach the heat supply and get burned. As is shown in the drawings on pages 19 and 21, "sunny" islands or spots can be created with the heat source, without illuminating the whole terrarium (see also Lighting, page 16).

Terrarium Technology

Bottom heating

If the terrarium is placed in an unheated room or if at night, after the heat is turned down, the necessary minimum temperature is not maintained, you must install a source of bottom heat (heating cable or heating mat, available in an electrical-supply, hardware, or appliance store.)

Gentle floor heating is also recommended if the necessary degree of humidity can't be maintained by frequent spraying of the plants. You can then spray the floor, and evaporation of the dampness will produce the proper humidity.

Caution: Observe to the letter the instructions for installing the heat source. Cover the heating cable with wire mesh made of stainless steel (wire gauge 0.2 to 0.4 inches [5 to 10mm]). This will avoid movement of or injury to the cable if the lizards dig in the ground. Only heating cables with low surface temperatures should be used. The roots of the terrarium plants are extremely sensitive to stored heat. To be on the safe side, you can wall off or insulate the plants with Styrofoam.

Heating in a water terrarium

Heating the terrarium floor from outside is simple, but so much energy is lost that it is

Water heater. It should be mounted in a hollow tile to keep the lizard from moving the heating rod or damaging it.

very inefficient. However, you can install a heatable filter or an aquarium heater. The heater must be mounted under the water surface in a perforated clay pipe or a hollow tile (see drawing). The lizards can't move the equipment and thus can't lift it out of the water or destroy it entirely.

Lighting

The diurnally active creatures of tropical climates will only be comfortable where there is sufficient bright light: Light as brightness has both a stimulating and a regulating effect on the nervous system. But light is not only brightness. It is composed of different colors, which are known as the range of the spectrum and which are measured in nanometers (nm). The visible spectrum lies between 380 and 780 nanometers; for plant growth a red portion of 650 to 700 nanometers is necessary, and lizards require radiation in the ultraviolet range (280 to 315 nanometers) for their metabolism of calcium. Since plants and animals have different light requirements, often the lighting of a terrarium can only be a compromise.

Fluorescent lamps are suitable as standard lighting for terrariums up to 28 inches (70 cm) in height. They are inexpensive to install and economical in use of power. Recommended are lamps that are high in the red end of the spectrum (for example Philips TL 83, OSRAM L 36, Vitalight, or Chroma 90 series). Such lamps produce satisfactory plant growth, and the color reflection of both plants and animals is satisfactory. Fluorescent lamps give off scarcely any heat. They should be changed after 6,000 hours. From this point on their light intensity decreases and the plants in the terrarium can no longer grow properly.

Spotlights (reflector lamps, see page 15) are most appropriate as warming-light sources but not for lighting the whole terrarium. The high heat output is damaging to lizards and plants. The ideal is a combination of fluorescent lights and spotlights. Using the spotlight you can create "sunny isles," distinctly warmer zones that are sufficiently far away from the plants.

Mercury vapor and halogen vapor lamps are only recommended for very large terrariums (at least 1.4 cubic yards [1 m³] in area). The light and heat output is so great that for the protection of plants and animals a space of at least 40 inches (1 m) must be allowed between the light and the contents of the terrarium. Furthermore, the colors will reflect unnaturally.

Ultraviolet Light

Ultraviolet (UV) lights stimulate biological responses. Essential for lizards are UV-B rays (280 to 315 nanometers), which control calcium metabolism, and UV-A rays (315 to 400 nanometers), which are very important for formation of pigment and vitamin D synthesis in the skin.

The combination of two fluorescent tubes with UV lamps — Philips TL 09 and TL 12 (20 and 40 watts) — has been proven good for maintenance and especially for the rearing of young lizards. The delivered strength of the combined rays is comparatively small. The fluorescent lamps can therefore be installed in the roof of a terrarium at least 20 inches (50 cm) high without danger of burning the lizards.

The OSRAM L/79 fluorescent light bulbs (20 to 100 watts) are especially effective in the UV-A band. The OSRAM Ultra-Vitalux (300 watts) is only appropriate for very large terrariums with a volume of at least 7 cubic yards (2 m³), where it is possible to maintain the necessary distance between light source and lizards.

Important: A period for getting used to UV radiation is absolutely necessary. Begin with an exposure of one minute only and lengthen the time daily by very small amounts, until after two months a time span of one hour has been reached.

Regulation of Temperature and Light

Most lizards must be kept cooler at night than during the day. For this reason you should install a thermostat and a timer in the terrarium. Choose a safe place for it, one where the animals can't touch it, thus changing the setting or damaging the instrument. The thermostat should not be placed in the direct path of beams from a warming lamp. It's advisable to couple the terrarium lighting mechanism to the timer as well. If the terrarium is located in a completely dark room, you should install a dimmer switch, otherwise, the sudden darkness or sudden light will frighten the lizards. With this type of setup, an adept lizard-keeper can control the light so that the "daytime activities" can be observed in the evening.

Terrarium Technology

Temperature control

Thermostats wear out with use and fail. Therefore the temperature in the terrarium must be monitored constantly. A simple indoor thermometer is satisfactory for this purpose and it can be installed inconspicuously. A minimum-maximum thermometer is recommended for temperature monitoring. This is especially important when the temperature of the terrarium can be influenced from outside, for example by sun streaming in.

Small and especially poorly ventilated terrariums can become overheated in such a short time that the animals inside die of heat prostration. If the danger of overheating cannot be ruled out absolutely, you must provide shade and a place for swimming.

Humidity control

The degree of relative humidity is measured by a hygrometer. Humidity is particularly important for lizards from regions of climatic extremes. This is as true for lizards from the tropical mountain forests, which nightly cooling makes damp and misty, as it is for lizards from the desert areas, which exhibit considerable humidity as a result of the nightly cooling — for short periods of time as much as 100 percent — and thus substantially more than can be achieved in most dry terrariums. The necessary humidity must be achieved through watering and spraying the plants or through moistening a gently heated ground surface.

Maintaining Water Purity

For mechanical filtering of large volumes of water (in water terrariums or bathing pools with brooks as inlets and outlets) you should install a motorized filter, which can be obtained in a pet store. The filtering materials usually supplied along with it are not necessary. Only the floss or the layers of various porous foam materials must be placed in the filter cannister. As soon as the filtering is finished, clean these materials by rinsing thoroughly in hot water. Use of a filter does not make changing the water unnecessary, however. Even clear water can be heavily polluted by the feces of the lizards.

Rain-Forest, Desert, and Water Terrariums

In the description of lizards that begins on page 62 you will find noted for each species of lizard the details of size and shape of terrarium as well as the materials for decorating it. The following descriptions of a rain forest, a desert, and a water habitat should give you additional help in shaping the proper environment for your lizards. Between the desert and the rain-forest habitat there is every imaginable transitional phase, so that obviously a terrarium can never be arranged "normally." The deciding factor is always the life style of the lizards you want to keep. Of basic importance is that the terrarium be well constructed, that is, territorial borders established for territorial lizards and all decorations and equipment details so arranged that cleaning the terrarium is possible without difficulty and the lizards can't be either pinched or injured.

The Rain-Forest Terrarium

The most noticeable features of a rain-forest terrarium are the luxuriously growing plants. They fulfill a decorative purpose and at the same time providing hunting-ground boundaries for territorial lizards.

Arrangement of back and side walls
A plant wall is appropriate when light values are sufficient. Screening of plastic or stainless-steel wire (mesh gauge 0.2 to 0.6 inches [0.5 to 1.5 cm]) is mounted so that there are 0.8 to 2 inches (2 to 5 cm) of space (depending on the size of the terrarium) between the wall and the screen. Fill this space with peat moss and sphagnum and press it down gently. The screening might be shaped a little as you

do this, so as to give the wall an interesting structure. Then cuttings of vines or hanging plants (see page 56) are stuck into the peat-sphagnum mixture and fastened with wire or plastic clips. Empty space can be filled in with peat or green sphagnum tips.
Walls masked with bark, bark planks, or bamboo provide the ideal environment for species that live primarily on tree tunks. Besides, they give your pets a much larger running area. The coverings should not furnish any unreachable hiding places for lizards or for food animals. Imitation woods of plastic are not suitable for terrariums.

If the terrarium walls are glass, they will be tinted with color on the outside; if the walls are of wood or Masonite they will be sealed on all sides (including the edges) with a plastic paint. These solutions are economical and hygienic.

Rain-forest terrarium built into a wall of bookshelves. Under the upper shelf: reflector lamp for heating the sunning spot, a fluorescent lamp for lighting, behind it an ultraviolet light (not shown here). A built-in terrarium must be extremely well ventilated (see page 12).

Rain-Forest, Desert, and Water Terrariums

Epiphytes and branches for climbing

If you are planning to use epiphytically growing plants in the terrarium (see page 56), you need the right kind of branches to hold the root balls. Branches of locust (Robinia) and lilac (Syringa) are especially suitable because the wood is not much injured by dampness. You can also use oak or the wood of stone-fruit trees. These kinds of wood are also suited for climbing branches. Evergreen branches do not have the interesting growth forms nor are they particularly long lasting. You must rule out the possibility of accidents (tipping or slipping branches, tails getting caught) by mounting the branches as follows:
● Cut the branches so that the cut surface will lie flat against the floor or the wall of the terrarium.
● Attach the branch by means of a metal corner and silicone caulk either to the glass floor or wall. If the wall is wood, you can use screws to fasten the branch firmly.
● Never mount branches so that they cross. Otherwise the lizards, especially long-tailed lizards, can catch their tails, thus injuring them.
● Don't introduce too many decorative materials or observation and access will be very difficult.

Floor medium

The nature of the floor material influences both the humidity of the floor and the air in the terrarium. A one- (or at most two-) year-old leaf or pine-needle surface, which in larger terrariums is covered with fresh-fallen leaves, is ideal. The ground-dwelling lizards can conceal themselves in this and, if they are not overfed, search in it for food. This particular type of food-seeking demonstrates

so much of lizard behavior that it justifies the additional effort to make frequent changes of leaves. (There is no other way to keep the terrarium clean.)

Water containers

In the rain-forest terrarium, a water container isn't necessary for most lizards. They drink the water that has collected in the "cisterns" of the bromeliads or in drops on the leaves of other plants.

Species that like to swim need a water bath. It must be large enough for the largest lizard living in the terrarium to fit comfortably into. A glass or a pottery container for example, is good. You can also model a small pond with epoxy resin bonded to fiberglass cloth, or you can make a running stream driven by a rotary pump.

The Desert Terrarium

In this type of terrarium — also called a dry terrarium — the stones are the most important element. With them you can construct natural-looking rocky terrains that offer plenty of display and hiding places for your lizards. The territorial behavior of the lizards makes it essential to structure the desert terrarium well. Often it is not possible to use living plants (see Planting zones, page 22) in the dry terrarium, so use a bunch of nonresinous driftwood or dried cholla cactus skeletons.

Decorations of natural stone

All kinds of sandstones and shales are recommended, since they can be worked easily and are found at most stonemasons. You can

20

Rain-Forest, Desert, and Water Terrariums

Desert terrarium with a display spot in the range of the warming light beam, a perforated side wall (left), and a top cover of wire screen.

easily shape them the way you want with the help of a cold chisel. But be careful using this tool; always wear safety glasses!

It will look the most natural if you only use stones of the same kind and from the same place.

Large stone constructions must be placed directly on the terrarium floor. Putting them on the sand is not secure enough; the lizards can tunnel under them, tip them over, and be injured. The single stones must be stuck to one another, because the lizards can also cause them to tumble down. You can use silicone caulk for gluing; you'll find it in a hardware or electrical-supply store, where you will find clear silicone that is safe to use in aquariums.

If you want to cover the back and the side walls with natural stone, build up the stones as regularly as possible — be careful about structure and arrangement — so that it looks like a hill of rock debris. The stones may be cemented together with freshly mixed mortar.

The mortar may be tinted to help create a more natural appearance.

Artificial stones

With a certain amount of handcrafting skill you can also shape deceptively real-looking stones out of fiberglass fabric bonded with epoxy or polyester resin.

Caution: Follow the manufacturer's instructions for handling the materials exactly so that you achieve the desired firmness and, above all, avoid any health hazards.

It's best to try making a sample first, so that you can try out the right colors and the appropriate surface. For instance, the "stone" should not be shiny, so you'll want to dull the surface with powder or sand. In doing so you should be careful not to make it too rough; otherwise the lizards can injure their feet on it.

Water containers

Lizards that can live in the dry terrarium don't as a rule need very large water baths. The amount of water necessary is small and is often found in a hollow in a stone, which you may work into it, if necessary.

Display places

You should create display places for dominant lizards. On the other hand, the lower-ranking animals need hiding places where they can escape the dominant animals and not be constantly overwhelmed by them.

Display places can easily be created from stones and dry wood (see drawing above). Make sure that these are going to be easy to make "sunny" later; that is, that they will lie in the angle of the warming light beam.

Rain-Forest, Desert, and Water Terrariums

For a *hiding place* you can use a cactus skeleton, which you may obtain in a pet shop. Otherwise you can lay a halved clay pipe on the sandy floor, being sure that its diameter is large enough. If you dampen the inside of such "caves" with a plant sprayer, your lizards will have cool, damp hiding places during the hot hours of the day and at night.

Whatever materials the caves or hiding places are made of, they must always be large enough so that a lizard won't become stuck inside and its hiding place become a prison. Also, the hiding places should be so arranged that they are accessible to you, or at the very least you can see into them.

Egg-laying places

Most eggs will be laid in the damp caves described above, for in nature such places provide both protection from hungry predators and the dampness necessary for the maturation (incubation) of the eggs. But you can also induce your lizards to lay eggs in a place you've prepared ahead of time. In that case, most of the floor of the terrarium is paved with brick or some other straight-sided stone and covered with a thin layer of sand, and the area planned for egg laying is left unpaved so that it has the depth necessary for burying the eggs. This area is filled with sand.

Planting zones

If the terrarium has an area of at least 5.4 square feet (0.5 m^2), it can be planted. Enough space must be left so that the UV and heat lamps can be arranged so as not to burn the plants.

Using a glass strip or a fence of stones, you can mark off a sufficiently large planting zone on the floor so that the plants can be well watered without soaking the whole floor. The fences should be fastened to the floor and the walls with silicone caulk. Since you will need to change the plants once in a while, they should be potted and the pots buried. The "fences" should be high enough so that the pots can't be seen. Cover the ground between the plant pots with a stainless-steel wire screen (mesh gauge, depending on the size of the lizards, 0.12 to 0.4 inches [3 to 10 mm]) to keep the lizards from digging in the damp area, for many lizards love to find damp resting places at night.

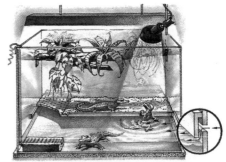

Water terrarium containing caimans. The epiphyte branches are mounted high enough so that the lizards can't climb on them and escape. (otherwise a screen cover is used). Bottom left: a hollow brick containing a water heater, with its lead wire threaded through a pipe. The detailed drawing shows a covered side vent, which prevents water leakage.

The Water Terrarium

For lizards that prefer to live in the water, such as water dragons, you must prepare a water (or aquatic) terrarium.

Rain-Forest, Desert, and Water Terrariums

Land portion

The land portion should be attached to the terrarium in the form of a shelf so that the animals will have the largest possible water surface at their disposal.

● For this you need a perforated polyvinyl-chloride (PVC) plate so that the water can drip through it.

● The plate should take up 35 to 40 percent of the area.

● The shelf should be mounted 0.8 inches (2 cm) over the surface of the water by means of side supports, which you can glue firmly to the side walls with silicone caulk.

● Attach a bead 0.8 to 1.2 inches (2 to 3 cm) high on the front edge.

● The shelf will be covered with coarse gravel which the raised edge will keep from rolling into the water.

● A heating rod is recommended for maintaining water temperature. It can be mounted in a hollow brick. The drawing on page 16 shows how to do it.

● You should install a motorized filter for mechanical purification of the water. This by no means avoids the necessity for a regular change of water!

Decoration

You can attach an epiphyte branch to the background or hang plants in appropriate pots for decoration. If the lizards are able to reach the branch, the terrarium must have a covering of wire mesh so that they cannot crawl out and escape.

Note: A side vent like the one shown in the drawing to the left is highly recommended.

Purchase and Quarantine

Endangered Species Regulations

Today many species of wild animals and plants are threatened by the destruction of habitats by fire, lumbering, use of insecticidal and herbicidal sprays, and not least, by hunting for the leather industry. In order to save what can still possibly be saved, an international agreement for the protection of endangered species, the Convention on International Trade in Endangered Species (CITES) of Wild Flora and Fauna (hereafter, the Washington Agreement or WA), was entered into on July 1, 1975, to regulate the traffic in living animals of those species designated endangered. Because a large number of reptiles are listed in the appendices to the WA, the agreement has considerable significance for reptile fanciers. The degree of endangerment of individual species varies, so the WA includes three appendices. An importer must see to it that the correct papers according to the appendix are provided for any sale that crosses international borders. A successful breeder of endangered species must register his breeding animals and offspring with an appropriate government office, usually an agricultural authority, and upon the sale of animals must pass on to the next owner a certificate, issued by that office.

There are additional state and federal regulations, as well as listings of endangered and threatened species that were not entirely covered by the WA. As a result not only is it difficult if not impossible to acquire such animals but the possessor of such animals is subject to special regulations.

As complicated as all this procedure seems, it is urgently advised that any possessor of protected species obey the regulations.

In some cases failure to do so is punishable by arrest, fine, and/or confiscation of the animal. The lizards included in the WA are designated in this book by the symbol * (see page 62).

Where You Buy Lizards

You can buy lizards in a pet store or from a breeder. In a good pet store you'll receive sound advice. Breeders will often offer lizards in herpetologist society journals and newsletters (see page 85). The number of males and females will be represented by two numbers separated by a comma: 1,2 means one male and two females; 0,3 means three females.

Important: Inspect the store or the breeding terrarium very carefully. They must be hygienically clean. You should not buy lizards from uncared-for or dirty terrariums.

Advice on Buying Lizards

Before choosing a lizard you should take plenty of time to observe the animals. Notice the following signs:

● The lizard must be in well-nourished condition: ribs, vertebrae, and pelvic bones should not show too noticeably under the skin and the eyes should not lie too deep in the head. Thighs and the root of the tail should look muscular, and skin in these areas should not have deep folds. During its active period the animals should be alert, with open eyes, observing what is going on in its surroundings. A healthy lizard reacts to disturbance with flight or tries to bite.

Purchase and Quarantine

• The mouth of the lizard should be closed. If it is always open a little at the back and bubbly froth can be seen around the mouth slit, at the openings to the nose, or around the eyes, the animal is unhealthy. In this case you shouldn't buy it.

• If the skin of the lizard exhibits pustules or lumps, very often systemic infections or skin mycoses may be responsible. Likewise, the metabolism is disturbed if molting is completed only with difficulty or the toes (especially frequent with geckos and skinks) have been constricted by molting problems. Such illnesses are difficult to treat, and you shouldn't buy an animal with these signs. Scars from bite wounds or a broken tail are beauty flaws that scarcely affect the animal.

• Watch out for external parasites. To do so, observe all the animals in the terrarium. If one animal is infested, most of the other animals will have parasites, too. A moderate attack of parasites will not injure a healthy lizard so much that you should refuse to buy it (see page 46).

Carrying Your Lizard Home

The pet store or the breeder will put the lizard in a linen bag for taking it home. In cool or cold weather, if the lizard is small, you can put it under your jacket, where the animal will be warmed by body heat. A large lizard will be put in its bag in a carton. In cool weather the carton should be made of Styrofoam. If it is very cold and there is a long way to go, you should protect the lizard with a hot-water bottle. But the temperature should not be higher than 90°F (32°C) because otherwise it could produce a concentration of warmth and lead to overheating.

Settling In

Before you put your newly acquired pet in a terrarium that is inhabited by other lizards, it should spend some time in a quarantine terrarium. There the lizard can get used to its new surroundings without having to undergo the pressure of territorial disputes with other animals. Furthermore, this is the only possible way for you to monitor the intake of food and carry out the necessary fecal examination (see page 26).

The quarantine terrarium

Prepare the quarantine terrarium before you buy the lizard. A discarded aquarium is quite suitable for this purpose. As a rule of thumb for the size, you can use about half the measurement given for your lizard species in the last chapter. The terrarium should be covered with a lid of wooden molding strips covered with fine wire screen. Side ventilation is not necessary. For lighting and heating use a reflector lamp or a heat lamp. You must install additional floor heating only if it gets too cold at night.

The arrangement: *Artificial Turf,* which is simple to clean and disinfect, is recommended as a floor covering. Besides, it serves some lizards as a cover. The humidity can be regulated if you dampen the absorbent mat as necessary. *Artificial Turf* isn't suitable for basilisks and agamas because these lizards get their claws caught in it. You can use shredded newspaper for these. Be aware, however, that the paper will be continually scuffled up by obstreperous lizards.

The drinking-water container can also serve as a bathing pool for those lizards who like to swim. Thus it should be large enough

25

so that the lizard can fit its whole body into it. For tree-dwellers you can place a branch in the terrarium for climbing; for shy and nervous animals a halved clay pipe, decorative cork, or nonresinous bark as places to hide.

If the lizard is especially uneasy, cover the front of the terrarium with a cloth or with paper. The curtain should only be removed when the animal has calmed down completely. If you want to be particularly cautious, you can take away the cloth or paper a little at a time and only remove it entirely after some days.

Maintenance note: If your lizard has ticks or mites, the animal must be treated in its transporting bag (see page 46) before it is placed in the quarantine terrarium.

First feeding

Herbivorous lizards can be offered leaves or fruit on the second day (see page 29).

Carnivorous lizards receive their first nourishment from four to seven days after their arrival. To excite their appetitie, put the food animals into the terrarium live. Don't put in too much at once, and observe the lizard. Mice, crickets, or roaches that are not eaten after several hours must be removed again, since they likely will not be eaten by the desolate lizard that is not yet acclimated to its changed environment.

Variety of proffered food is especially important at this time. Different colors and smells of vegetable food and the various movements of live food animals can awaken the appetite of your pet. Take time during the acclimatizing phase to observe your lizard. This way you will learn how much food it needs. If the animal rejects food for longer than two weeks and visibly loses weight during this period, it must be force-fed (see page 30).

Quarantine procedures

During quarantine the feces of the lizard must be examined.

● If the feces are viscous and have a penetrating smell — normal for the fish-eating monitor lizards — an inflammation of the digestive tract is usually the cause (see page 49).

● Bloody feces — not to be confused with the red color after a feeding with grasshoppers — indicate an injury to the intestine.

● If you find worms in the feces, you must collect them and have them examined by a veterinarian. A worm infestation is also possible if no worms are found, however. Therefore the veterinarian should be given the freshest possible fecal sample. Only he or she can determine if worm eggs are present and start treatment if necessary (see page 52).

Feeding

The eating habits of lizards vary as widely from species to species as do the habitats. There are lizards that eat animal food or a plant diet exclusively. Some species live on plants as well as animal prey. In any case, whichever lizard you are keeping, providing as much variety in the diet as possible is extremely important because that is the only way the animals will receive sufficient amounts of the necessary vitamins and minerals (see page 28).

Plant Food

For the plant-eating lizards, the most valuable foods are wild grasses and weeds. Among these are, for example, dandelion, plantain, clover, and chickweed. You can gather the weeds yourself, but don't take them from along the edge of a highly traveled road: the level of polluting materials on the plants would be too high. Fruit and vegetables from your own garden — those treated with as little commercial fertilizer and pesticides as possible — are also valuable foods.

Especially important in addition are: citrus fruit and sweet red peppers (high in vitamin C), carrots (contain important precursors for Vitamin A), spinach and kale (rich in vitamin B and minerals). If you don't have your own garden, you should take care to buy naturally raised and ripened fruits and vegetables as much as possible. For instance, bananas that are harvested green in the tropics and then artificially ripened in transit or after arrival at the market are less nutritious than plums or strawberries that have been naturally ripened nearby. In the same way, the untreated and perhaps therefore spotty, wormy apple is preferable to the sprayed and waxed one. In the winter months it is especially difficult to provide the lizards with fresh food. Cooked unpolished brown rice that has been made tasty with bananas or apples, diced small, or unsulfured figs, dates, and raisins has proven to be a good variation during the cold months. To avoid any deficiency diseases, the rice-and-fruit mixture should be enriched with vitamin and mineral supplements (see Food Supplements page 29).

Animal Food

Lizards that eat animal food also need as varied a diet as possible to remain healthy. The data in the descriptions of specific lizards (page 62) should help you to fulfill the diet requirements of your pets.

Freshwater fish

A long list of lizard species love fish. Never offer fish filleted — only whole, with scales, bones, entrails, stomach contents and all, to ensure provision of a continued supply of vitamin and mineral elements. You can buy fish of various sizes for feeding in pet stores. If you know a fisherman, perhaps you can get some of his catch once in a while. Make sure that the fish comes from water that is as unpolluted as possible. Pollutants can collect in the tissues of reptiles and cause injury to their inner organs. If you have a freezer, you can freeze fish to have some in reserve. Follow the recommended procedure for the storing of table fish.

Feeding

Snails and worms

In damp weather you can collect slugs and small snails (*Cepaea* species and *Helix aspersa)*, which for some skinks (see page 77) are the preferred or only food. These mollusks can be kept in a closed container, sufficiently large and with air holes in it, in a cool room or in a refrigerator for three to four weeks. Some lizards will also gladly accept earthworms. These can be dug up or collected on warm rainy days. Gardeners can find the worms in compost heaps. But you can also buy them in bait-and-tackle shops.

Insects, spiders, small mammals

Many insects and spiders (arachnids) can be caught with a net, for example on weedy vacant lots. But you may not net insects in protected areas and you are not allowed to have any protected species in your catch. Information about conservation laws and regulations can be obtained from your community or state authorities or from conservation groups. Since these conservation regulations change often, you should keep yourself currently informed.

For the young of any species of small lizard, plant lice (aphids) — offered with the leaves and branch on which the insects live — are suitable food. You can also buy food insects or small mammals (mice and rats for the larger lizards) in a pet store. There are also farms that specialize in raising food animals. You can get the food for your animals from these by subscription.

Vitamins

Vitamins are life-supporting elements that the lizard body either cannot make or cannot make enough of because of living in a terrarium. They must thus be added to the diet. Vitamins perform various functions:

- Vitamin A is important for vision and for skin and gland maintenance. In addition it influences growth, the immune system, and fertility.
- Vitamins in the B group are important for the utilization of plant and animal protein and influence the metabolism of nerve cells and cell division.
- Vitamin C is important in defense against infectious diseases.
- Vitamins in the D group promote bone growth and maintenance.
- Vitamin E plays a role in muscle development and is significant in the birth and egg-laying processes.
- Vitamin K is important for blood clotting.

Minerals

The minerals that are essential for lizards include calcium, magnesium, phosphorus, and potassium. They are primarily used for the development of teeth and bones. Therefore enough of them must be provided, above all for young animals still in their growth period. If young animals do not receive enough minerals (see Proper Feeding, page 29), rickets may result.

Female lizards, especially, require increased mineral intake for the production of eggs and their shells.

Trace elements — recognized ones include iron, iodine, fluorine, and selenium — are involved, for example, in the production of enzymes and hormones.

Mineral supplements, if required, are added to the food like vitamin supplements.

Feeding

Proper Feeding

Diurnal (daytime-active) lizards are fed during the course of the day or else during the day phase that is established by the time clock. Nocturnal (nighttime-active) lizards receive their food toward evening.

Feeding herbivorous lizards

Rice and cut-up fruit and vegetables are offered in a bowl. It should be made of glass or pottery, especially for the big lizards. Lightweight plastic bowls may tip if the animal should step on them while eating.

Weeds, grasses, and leaf vegetables can be laid on the floor of the terrarium. If there are several lizards, you should lay the greens in different places so that the lower-ranking animals will also find the food.

Food supplements are not necessary for herbivorous lizards during the summer months if there are enough naturally ripened weeds, fruit, and vegetables available. During the times when vegetation is scarce, you must add a vitamin-mineral supplement (for example, Vionate or Pervinal). Because these change the appearance, taste, and smell of the food, you must accustom the lizards to them by slowly increasing dosage.

An effective and economical calcium source is available in crushed eggshells or cuttlebone, which are well liked by many lizards.

Feeding carnivorous lizards

Slugs and small snails with shells may be put into the terrarium alive in small quantities. The lizards like to crack open the shells by themselves. Large edible snails should be scalded before being fed to lizards, shells removed, and be cut up.

Plant lice can be placed in the terrarium still on the plants and leaves on which they are found.

Living insects should be thrown to the particular lizard so that the insect is eaten as soon as possible. Escaped crickets disturb the lizard-keeper and his neighbors with their nightly chirping. Besides, the uneaten insects can eat the plants and even bite the lizards.

To avoid this, the lizard can be accustomed to receiving the living insect with tweezers. Or the insect may be scalded before it is fed to the lizard. Roaches should be scalded before being fed in any case (see page 32).

Mice and rats should be killed and offered with tweezers. Living animals can be tormented when they are hunted by the lizard. Only during the acclimation period for newly acquired lizards should you place living food animals in the terrarium. The movements of the prey excite the lizards' appetite.

Caution: Animals that have been removed from the freezer must be warmed enough before feeding so that they reach room temperature all the way through.

Food supplements must also be given to carnivorous lizards. If living insects are being used, put the cricket or grasshopper in a closed box (or a plastic bag) in which you have put a pinch of vitamin-and-mineral supplement beforehand. The box or bag is then shaken hard, and the "floured" insect is fed right away so that it can't shake the powder off again. For large lizards, the vitamin-and-mineral supplements can be sprayed in the abdominal cavities of dead mice, rats, or fish. Smaller lizards, which ingest their daily

Feeding

drinking water drop by drop, are given their vitamins in drinking water.

Some lizards are also very fond of crushed eggshells or cuttlebone (calcium). Try out different grain sizes.

Don't try to force the food supplements into your lizards under pressure. The stress produced by being caught and having the mouth forced open can do more harm than the vitamin and mineral intake would do good. Such measures should be used only when the animal must be caught and force-fed or treated anyway.

Many minerals not needed by the lizard's body will be excreted in the urine. Calcium deposits on the interior organs are not, as is often wrongly supposed, due to the intake of too much mineral supplement but to metabolic disturbances and overdosage of vitamin D.

Force-Feeding

A lizard that has refused food for a long time must be force-fed. You can hold a small lizard in your left hand (see drawing at right) and open the mouth of the animal with your right hand. For a larger lizard you need someone to help you. While one person holds the lizard (see drawing on page 46), the other must try to open the mouth of the animal. If there is a dewlap or enough skin in the under jaw, the lizard may be grasped there and the mouth opened with a steady pull. For animals that have no dewlap or skin folds, press a fingernail or plastic kitchen spatula in the backmost corner of the mouth between the teeth and block the jaw open. To keep the

mouth open, press two fingers in the corner of the lizard's mouth with a firm grip. Or you can lay a plastic spatula or a piece of rubber tubing there.

Caution: Never use a metal lever to pry open and block the jaw; you will injure the lizard with it!

Carnivorous lizards receive a fish, a squashed cricket, or a young mouse. Animals with fur should be lubricated with raw egg white so that they will slide down more easily. You can give herbivorous lizards fruit and edible tender leaves. Wait a while to see if the lizard swallows the food. If this does not happen, you must introduce the animal or the vegetable morsel deep into the throat. But be very careful doing it!

Forced feeding is repeated up to three times at intervals of several days. Change the food often so as to stimulate the lizard's appetite. If you are not successful in inducing the animal to feed within seven to ten days, have it examined by a veterinarian.

Force-feeding a caiman. The mouth is wedged open with a piece of rubber tubing. During feeding the soft palate is pressed frontward so that the fish can be pushed into the esophagus.

Keeping and Breeding Food Animals

The best insects to breed for food are crickets, grasshoppers, and cockroaches. Other insects that are difficult to get or to breed are too demanding for the beginning terrarium-keeper. If you are interested all the same, consult the reference list (see below).

Insects

Crickets (*Acheta domestica* and *Gryllus bimaculatus*)
Excellent for breeding.
Mormon cricket *(Anabus simplex)*
Less productive than other cricket species; nevertheless, recommended for variety.
Camel cricket *(Ceuthophilus)* and the North American *Nemobius*.
Maintenance: For enough of a supply for small lizards, a 1.2-cubic-yard (40-liter) aquarium, closed with a cover of fine wire or plastic screen.
Equipment: Paper cylinders and egg cartons, which increase the running area and provide cover. They must be replaced as soon as they are dirtied with the excrement of the crickets. Use a bird-cage water holder for a water container.
Food: Apples, carrots, green leaves. Dog kibble is especially suitable because it is enriched with vitamins. Add multivitamin preparation to the drinking water (0.07 ounces per quart [2 ml/L]).
Breeding: Laying dishes — for example, 1-quart (1-liter) plastic storage boxes — filled with a soft, damp, spongy mixture of peat moss and sand, leafmold, or pine needles should be placed in the breeding cage. If you need many crickets, the laying dishes should be transferred to a rearing container once a week. Then in every rearing container there will be crickets of approximately the same size, which will avoid time wasted in sorting them later. If you have only a small rearing container — which is enough for a small crop of insects — the crickets must be sorted according to size at feeding time. The opening to the drinking-water container should be closed with a swab of cotton so the young crickets can't drown.
Temperature: 77 – 86°F (25 – 30°C). Place container in a heated area, on a heating cable or heating pad, or on top of a fluorescent light fixture.

Grasshoppers (*Romalea microptera; Dissosteira, Melanopus*)
Also an excellent food insect, considerably larger than crickets. However, they require a higher consumption of electricity and demand more time than crickets.
Warning: People who are allergic to pollen should not keep or breed grasshoppers!
Maintenance: Cage $20 \times 16 \times 20$ inches $(50 \times 40 \times 50$ cm), ventilated by means of wire screening either as a cover or built into a side wall. Stagnant air, particularly when humid, is bad for breeding. Since the grasshoppers can jump quite far, it is recommended that a small trap door or sliding door (at most 5×5 inches [12×12 cm]) that will only allow passage of the keeper's hand and arm be fixed on the cage.
Equipment: Sliding trays of perforated tin permit hygienic maintenance: the feces and urine can fall through the holes and be removed easily from the shelf underneath. Crumpled wire screening can be used as a frame for climbing.

Keeping and Breeding Food Animals

Feeding: Grass, 4- to 6-inch- (10- to 15-cm-) long wheat shoots — but be careful, because a sudden change of food leads to diarrhea; make changes gradually! In addition, white clover and wheat-shoot clippings enriched with a vitamin-mineral supplement.

Breeding: Cut one or two openings about 4 × 4 inches (10 × 10 cm) large in the tin floor; under it slide a laying tray at least 4 inches (10 cm) high.

Egg-laying medium: Soft, damp mixture of peat moss, sand, and leaf- or pine-needle mold. Transfer the laying trays weekly to a separate breeding and raising cage, which can be smaller than the cage for the breeding insects. The perforations in the floor should not be larger than 0.04 inches (1 mm) or the freshly hatched grasshoppers may slip through. For optimum use of space, use a piece of crumpled wire screening as a climbing structure.

Temperature: 83 – 95°F (28 – 35°C). Place a heating cable or pad under the cage. As a source of heat and light, install an incandescent bulb in the cage and turn this off in the evening. Temperature changes between day and night make the grasshoppers hardier.

American cockroach *(Periplaneta americana)*
Oriental cockroach *(Blatta orientalis)*
German cockroach *(Blatella germanica)*
    Very adaptable and reproduces well; therefore its recommendation is limited only because escaped roaches quickly become a plague in the house!

Maintenance: Like crickets, but need more places to hide, such as paper tubes and egg cartons.

Feeding: Like crickets but give them more fruit.

Breeding: Like crickets, but laying trays are not necessary; egg bundles will be laid on floor or in hiding places. Transfer of eggs into rearing cages is not necessary.

Note: Scald the roaches before feeding them to lizards so that they can't escape.

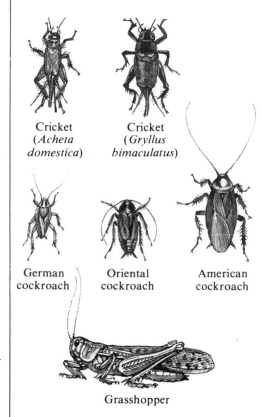

Cricket
(Acheta domestica)

Cricket
(Gryllus bimaculatus)

German cockroach

Oriental cockroach

American cockroach

Grasshopper

Food insect for the lizards that need animal nourishment:

Keeping and Breeding Food Animals

Small Mammals

If you keep large lizards, it is worthwhile to breed mice or rats. But even for the middle-sized, insect-eating lizards a feeding of baby mice can provide a welcome change. Breeding these rodents offers scarcely any difficulties if a cage arrangement like those in laboratories or at large-scale breeders (such as pet stores) is used.

Mice

Maintenance: Cage area 16 × 10 inches (40 × 25 cm) for one male, six females, and young. Using more breeding animals is not recommended because the mother animals may be disturbed by the resulting commotion. Result: premature births, too little production of milk, gnawing and eating of newborn. Use wood chips for bedding material, dust-free so as not to irritate the mucous membranes of nose and mouth. Renew chips often. Ensure sufficient ventilation with fresh air. Position of the cage: in an easily ventilated area at a temperature of at least 65°F (18°C).

Feeding: Special food for rodents, specifically Rat and Mouse Feed, available in agricultural-supply stores, feed stores, and pet shops. Kitchen scraps are not adequate!

Reproduction: Gestation period 20 to 22 days. Usually 6 to 10 young per litter; in exceptional circumstances as many as 20. Females will be receptive again one day after delivery, so a new litter may be expected after three weeks. Within 12 to 15 months — after this time breeding animals should be changed — a female can bear as many as 150 young.

Rats

Maintenance: Cage area 16 × 10 inches (40 × 25 cm) for one male, two females, and young. More breeding animals will require correspondingly more space. Position, bedding, and feeding like those of mice.

Reproduction: Gestation period 21 days; but it can last as long as five weeks if an especially large litter is still nursing. Usually 9 to 12 per litter, rarely 20 and more young. After 15 months the breeding animals should be changed; until then 100 to 120 offspring can be expected.

Basic Care and Maintenance

Important Rules for the Lizard-Keeper

The rules given below for the care and maintenance of lizards belong to the basic knowledge of every lizard-keeper. They are rules that retain their worth and importance as long as you care for lizards.

● Before you buy a lizard, inform yourself about its particular life requirements in the terrarium. You must also be knowledgeable about the requirements for living space, climate, and food of the chosen lizard species.

● You should never forget that lizards are wild animals that need no petting but do need the expert knowledge of the keeper.

● All maintenance measures must be carefully carried out. Hygiene affects not only the health of the lizards but also protects the keeper from possible damage to his or her own health.

● The terrarium, whether one or a group of several, must be arranged to be observable because this facilitates routine maintenance.

● Technical installations and arrangements must be so planned, installed, and maintained that neither animal nor human can come to harm (see Avoiding Electrical Accidents, page 15).

● It is important to observe the lizards carefully and often enough to notice any changes in behavior or appearance as soon as possible. Otherwise you will be unable to come to assistance promptly, for example, at the beginning of an illness or refusal of food.

● Always be conscious of the responsibility that you have undertaken in keeping the animals.

Note: If you want to keep the more frightening lizards — such as large iguanas — or want to raise food animals that might annoy the neighbors by noise or smell (see pages 29 and 32), you should obtain permission from your landlord.

Controlling the Climate in the Terrarium

Since lizards cannot produce their own warmth (see page 5), they are dependent upon the correct temperature in their environment. The lizard-keeper must therefore try to create the best possible appropriate climatic conditions for this type of lizard. Besides temperature, climate includes humidity, precipitation, light, and air pressure. Moreover, the rhythm in which these occur in the change of seasons and between day and night has a crucial effect on the lizard. This means that you must constantly control these factors and must adjust the circumstances of daytime and season. The change from day to nighttime climate is extremely important, because it profoundly affects the vitality of the lizards. An appropriate climate in the terrarium can only be created and maintained with the help of technical apparatus (see Terrarium Technology, page 15). The required humidity will be achieved in the planted rain-forest terrarium by watering or else by the daily spraying of the plants. In the unplanted terrarium the ground may be dampened with a spray bottle

Iguanas and agamas. Top: Common iguana *(Iguana iguana)* with unusually high comb; bottom left: angle-headed lizard *(Acanthosaura crucigera)*; right: Oriental (Chinese) water dragon *(Physignathus concincinus)*, male.

Basic Care and Maintenance

and, if necessary, gently heated so that the desired humidity will result from steady evaporation. The humidifiers sold in stores are only suitable for very large terrariums.
Note: Without fail, monitor the required air circulation in the terrarium (see Ventilation, page 12).

Cleaning the Terrarium

Not only for aesthetic reasons but even more for hygienic ones, the urine and feces of the lizards must be removed from the terrarium as soon as possible. The floor medium must therefore be renewed as the occasion demands. The interval necessary between cleanings or changes of floor medium depends on the size and number of the lizards being kept, so it isn't possible to give an exact rule. A lizard-keeper who observes the terrarium daily will quickly determine how often cleaning is necessary to keep any bad odor from occurring.

A simple arrangement of decorations is recommended to make it possible to carry out the work of cleaning quickly and thoroughly. The proper equipment is also important: you need sponges, brushes, a scoop, and tweezers.

Geckos. Top left: Adult leopard gecko *(Eublepharis macularis)*; top right: young panther gecko, still unspotted, with broad dark-brown striped bands; middle left: Madagascar gecko *(Phelsuma madagascariensis)*; middle right: gold dust madagascar day gecko *(Phelsuma laticauda)*; bottom left: Asiatic house gecko *(Hemidactylus frenatus)*; bottom right; Tokay gecko *(Gecko gecko)*.

You can also use the same tweezers, thoroughly cleaned, as feeding tweezers.

The equipment should be cleaned as thoroughly as possible after each use — preferably under household bleach and running hot water. Disinfecting it between uses is highly recommended.

Care of several terrariums

Hygienic principles are particularly important if you have to tend more than one terrarium, because the danger of an infection or the transfer of a parasite infestation can't then be excluded. Therefore you should observe the following maintenance procedures:

● You need separate cleaning utensils for each terrarium.

● The equipment should be disinfected after each use.

● Choose a volatile, i.e., a fast-evaporating disinfectant because a relatively long rinsing time will be required for others to avoid any residue. Decoration materials must be disinfected especially thoroughly if you take them out of one terrarium for use in another. Disinfection is even more essential after the death of a lizard!

● Remainders of food or of food animals that have not been eaten by the lizards should under no circumstances be used to feed animals in another terrarium. If you don't want to throw remainders out, then the second time around use them only in the same terrarium.

● Plants that have been removed from a terrarium should be cared for outside it for a time (several months) before being replanted inside.

37

Basic Care and Maintenance

Body-Care Procedures

You will only have recourse to these procedures for body care in unusual circumstances.

Removal of remaining skin
Most lizards accomplish their molting without any difficulty; occasionally the keeper must remove the remaining portions of the old skin.

In very rare instances — most often resulting from insufficient humidity — some skin will remain at the ends of the toes. If such remainders dry out, they can constrict the toes so tightly that a portion of them can be lost. You must avoid this; soak the foot briefly in warm water or allow the lizard to run on damp *bath toweling* and then remove the skin.

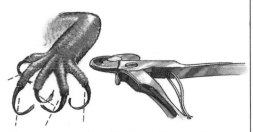

Place to cut   Special claw-clipping shears

Cutting the claws. Only ground-dwellin lizards should have their claws clipped.

Cutting claws
Long, sharp claws are typical for many species and ought not to be cut. But with ground-dwelling lizards they may become long and curved because the floor material is artificial or the animal isn't active enough, and then they must be clipped. The drawing above shows how to cut properly. Be careful not to cut into the part of the claw where there is blood circulation. As a beginner, you should probably have the claw-cutting done the first time by a veterinarian, an experienced pet-shop owner, or another lizard fancier.

Holding Lizards Properly

To be able to do claw-cutting, force-feeding, or treatment procedures in case of illness, it is usually necessary to take the lizard in your hand and hold it so that neither human nor lizard can come to harm.

Small to medium-large lizards must be grasped quickly and with sure aim. Thumb and forefinger of the dominant hand hold the lizard behind the head and fix it so that it

Holding a small lizard. Grasp the animal with both hands. Thumb and forefinger of the left hand must fix the head to keep the lizard from biting.

can't bite. The palm lies on the lizard's back, the three free fingers grasp the legs from underneath and fix them toward the back-swept hips and tail. Thus the lizard cannot bite and scratch, and it is not in danger of shedding its tail or injuring it by wild thrashing. The necessary measures can then be administered with the other hand.

Larger lizards can scarcely be held and treated by one person alone; a helper is necessary. The keeper holds the neck with the nondominant hand and thus fixes the head and the forward extremities; the dominant hand grasps the tail area and thereby holds the rear extremities at the same time (see drawing on page 46). For a large and aggressive lizard, the tail must also be fixed by being grasped firmly between the keeper's legs. All the necessary ministrations to the lizard are carried out by the second person.

Avoiding Stress Situations in the Terrarium

Only someone who observes his lizards regularly and knows how they behave can judge promptly whether a lizard in a terrarium is undergoing a stress situation. If a lizard is constantly threatened by one of the others or if an animal shows the submissive behavior pattern too often — for example, treading (see page 11) — the keeper must intervene quickly. Otherwise the dominated lizard will languish and can even die in such circumstances. By building up the decorations, you can erect barriers that provide the dominated animal with its own territory. If this is not possible because the terrarium isn't big enough, the only thing that will help is separating the lizards.

You should by all means avoid introducing a new animal into a terrarium in which the inhabitants have already established their own territories. The new animal will soon suffer submission stress. If the introduction of the new inhabitant cannot be avoided for some reason, it is recommended that the original animals be removed and only replaced after the new one has become acclimated. Usually old inhabitants can still dominate because it recognizes the familiar surroundings; in this case rearrangement of the terrarium is the only help.

Mixing of several different species can also produce a stress situation. Basically you should provide each lizard type with its own living space. In sufficiently large terrariums — or in a greenhouse — some kinds can be mixed together. A prerequisite for this is that the lizards be about the same size and that no personal antipathies (there are such things with lizards, too) can be observed. Very

Adhesive lamellae on the toes of a tokay (enlarged at right). Microscopic hook cells on the lamellae allow the tokay to maintain its hold even on a vertical plate of glass.

Basic Care and Maintenance

close and regular observation is extraordinarily important in any mixing situation because a dominated lizard can quickly disappear into a difficult-to-see corner. Those lizards that can be mixed with others are listed in the last chapter (page 62).

Anyone planning to mix several kinds of lizards should start out with an entirely new terrarium. The disruption of "household peace" by a dominant lizard strengthened by a sense of territorial possession will then be ruled out ahead of time.

Care of Your Lizards When You Go on Vacation

The care of a lizard terrarium during vacation time is relatively simple if you find a responsible person who can look at the terrarium occasionally. Naturally it would be best if another keeper of terrarium animals could take over.

In any case, the vacation replacement must be well instructed, for even an experienced terrarium-keeper must get to know his charges beforehand and be able to focus on individual details. Above all he must make himself familiar with the technical equipment ahead of time so that he can deal quickly with any failures. Before your departure you should make arrangements that will somewhat ease the duties for your replacement.

● Place the terrarium so that there are no possible outside influences on the temperature inside it — for instance, by sunlight falling on it, which might result in dangerous overheating.

● To induce a phase of decreased activity in the lizards, the temperature in the terrarium can be reduced by 9°F (5°C) by, for example, not turning on the heating lamp or the spots. In this way any possible aggressive behavior will be checked and also the lizards' energy needs will be reduced considerably so that they need not be fed and the excrement will not collect as often as under conditions of optimum temperature.

● Tell your substitute that the provision of drinking water and the watering of plants is important. Because of the lowered temperature and the resulting lower evaporation rate, these measures are only necessary at wide intervals, to be sure, but they must not be neglected. With a well-informed vacation replacement and the above rules, your lizards can last out a three-week vacation unharmed.

Introduction to Lizard Breeding

Many lizard fanciers will want to get their lizards to breed. On the one hand, successful breeding is reassurance that you have created optimal living conditions for the animals, for if the conditions are not right, you will certainly be unsuccessful. On the other hand, by raising healthy offspring, you contribute to the conservation of lizards living in the wild.

The Parent Animals

As a rule you need a breeding pair if you are going to try to breed, but sometimes it can happen that you acquire a pregnant female. Care of this female requires meticulous attention because the capture, transport, and changes of environment and climate are particularly damaging to a pregnant animal; successful egg-laying will only occur under the best possible environmental conditions.

Most lizard-keepers are not acquainted with the phenomenon that can occur in some lizard populations: unisexual reproduction (parthenogenesis); it is considered an exception. Therefore the lizard-keeper must become concerned with distinguishing between male and female.

Determination of sex

For lizards with distinct dimorphism, that is with visible distinctions between male and female, determining sex by external markings of mature animals is easy. It is more difficult or impossible with the young animals of these species, for instance the Canary Island lizard and Weber's sailing lizard. With the beginning of sexual maturity, the males of some species of lizards grow flaps of skin or combs of varying sizes on their heads, throats, backs, or tails. In other groups the males, always or only during the mating season, are of a noticeably brighter color than the female. Constant and clearly visible marks of difference are the two large scales behind the cloaca of male anoles, the anal or preanal pores (see drawing below) of geckos, and the thigh or femoral pores of the agamas, and most iguanid species. Preanal or femoral pores — in some genera both — are mostly present in males but are also observable in the females of some species, although always significantly less noticeable. For definite determination, lizards of about the same size or about the same age should be available for comparison.

Much experience enables a lizard fancier to determine sex from skull proportions and length, breadth, or circumference of the root of the tail. Lizard-keepers who would like to know more about this should learn from an experienced lizard-keeper.

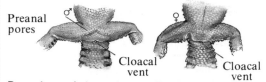

Preanal pores Cloacal vent Cloacal vent

Preanal pores in leopard gecko. They are always found in this position. (♂ = male, ♀ = female)

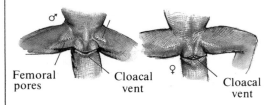

Femoral pores Cloacal vent Cloacal vent

Femoral pores of the Oriental water dragon. In other species they may be arranged along the entire length of the upper thigh.

Introduction to Lizard Breeding

Modes of determining sex

With many lizards, sex determination is only possible through the use of a probe. How to hold the probe is difficult to describe and would be a digression in this book. The examination requires a great deal of experience and empathetic concern, so that for the first time you should have the counsel and help of an experienced lizard-keeper. You may contact other lizard fanciers through the various lizard-fanciers organizations (see Addresses, page 85).

Prerequisites for Mating

Unfortunately, possession of definitely identified, optimally cared-for males and females does not guarantee successful mating; the stimulation of sexual instinct is the deciding factor. Climate is an important trigger. It plays a great role, especially with the lizards who live in the climatically moderate zones of the northern and southern hemispheres of our earth. As soon as the dark, cold winter months are over, these lizards begin the mating period immediately after leaving winter quarters. In the areas near the equator, the unbearably hot time of the year can induce a resting phase. To make triggering of the sexual drive possible in the terrarium, you must be able to control the climate effectively. Thus it is essential that you know as much as possible about the origins of the lizards and their climate needs.

Courtship

Many forms of courtship are observable at mating time. Iguanas present their dewlap while nodding their heads. Agamas also nod their heads and "wave" at the same time — that is, they execute a circular horizontal movement with a front leg. Male anoles woo a female with a quick nodding of the head.

The lizards may take almost no nourishment during the courtship period, in spite of their activity, but there is no cause for worry if they have been as well nourished as possible beforehand. Eating will follow later and often at an above-average rate for the female, who should be left along during this period, because the production of eggs demands an above-average supply of energy.

Mating

The intromittent sexual organs of male reptiles are concealed in the external opening of the cloaca, which is covered by the transverse flaplike vent in all lizards. Male lizards possess paired organs called hemipenes which lie within sheaths in the ventral portion of the tail. Each hemipenis is connected to a testicle by a tubular vas deferens. The testicles are located within the body cavity and lie near the kidneys.

It is anatomically impossible for male lizards to mount for copulation as do the mammals. They approach the female from the side; the males of many lizard species bite the neck of the female and try to maneuver the cloaca as close as possible to that of the female. Then the hemipenis that is nearest to the opening of the female's cloaca is erected. The hemipenes of the various species of lizards, which are creased or grooved in a variety of ways that are type-specific to each species, are provided with thorns or barbs,

Introduction to Lizard Breeding

A pair of blue-tongued skinks mating. The male grasps the female with a bite on the neck.

thus making possible secure binding during mating. The sperm flows through the tube-shaped penis in a channel along the hemipenis to the cloaca of the female. There it enters the oviducts where fertilization occurs. With some reptiles, sperm can be stockpiled by the female so that fertilization of late-maturing eggs can still take place after months or years.

Egg-Laying

As the day of egg-laying nears, the female will inspect the ground surface and dig holes in many places. She will do it as often and as long as it takes until one of these test holes meets with her approval; then egg-laying begins. In most cases the eggs must be transferred to an incubator. But this should not be done before the female has finished laying her eggs and has covered over the nest hole again. Any intervention too soon is a disturbance and can result in discontinuance of the laying and may cause a laying emergency as a consequence!

Transferring the Eggs to the Incubator

An incubator is necessary for brooding the eggs (maturing or incubation). It should have been set up during the courtship period and be standing ready. A discarded aquarium or a small refrigerator that no longer works are suitable for use as incubators. A thermostatically controlled heat source (a heating cable, heat lamp, or incandescent bulb) must be installed inside. You will find details of incubator temperature and length of incubation in the descriptions of the lizards in the last chapter. Before transferring the eggs, you must be sure that the proper temperature has been reached and that it can be maintained constantly.

You need a container for the clutch of eggs — a refrigerator box is best for this. It should be filled with vermiculite, mica that has been fired to become heat-resistant (available in pet and garden shops). Vermiculite comes in various grain sizes; the best mixture is vermiculite No. 3 VET mixed with water in a proportion ranging from 1:1.5 parts to 1:2 parts by weight. This gives you a material of the proper dampness, which will remain that way in the closed refrigerator container.

Transferring the eggs

After the egg-laying is completed, carefully uncover the nest hole and remove the clutch. Unearthing must be undertaken with special care because the eggs of most lizards have a flexible shell, something like a soft plastic — only that of most geckos is hardened by deposited calcium. You must also be careful not to change the position of the eggs while

Introduction to Lizard Breeding

A displaying anole. Display with erected dewlap is typical of the anole species.

removing them. In nature, in contrast to birds, reptile eggs are not moved again after they are laid; the embryo is fixed and may be smothered by the yolk supply if the position of the egg is later changed. After the eggs are settled into the incubating medium, the box is closed so that a minimal amount of air circulation is possible, and then it is placed in . the incubator. If you are using vermiculite as a hatching medium, the often-recommended examination and removal of unfruitful eggs is not necessary. Such measures only cause damage, particularly as experience has shown that healthy eggs are not harmed by dead ones. Also unnecessary is the so-frequently recommended evaporation of water to maintain a high level of relative humidity in the incubator. In a closed refrigerator container the desired humidity is maintained!

The Young Animal

How long the eggs remain in the incubator depends on the species of lizard. The matu-ration time, the length of time between egg-laying and hatching, can vary widely. For instance, with monitor lizards it requires up to 120 days, whereas it is only 50 days for the Madagascar gecko. To free itself from the egg, the hatchling uses its egg tooth to rip open the shell. This is a tooth, located forward on the premaxillary bone, which grows in most lizard embryos and falls out a few days after hatching. After hatching, the young lizards are placed in a separate terrarium, arranged appropriately for the species of lizard. In the "parental" terrarium they would be in danger of attack and resulting fatal bites from the parent animals. The newly hatched lizards must slowly become used to the climate of the parent animals after the regular temperature of the incubator. There is no reason to keep them warmer. Any unnecessarily higher temperature — especially the failure to lower the temperature at night — does certainly allow the young to grow more quickly, but the negative consequences also show quickly. The calcium cannot be maintained and rickets or other metabolic bone diseases (see page 48) result; also vitamin B complex deficiencies may develop, convulsive trembling results (see page 48), and soon the promising offspring have become miserable objects of pity.

Ultraviolet irradiation is required for the successful raising of many lizards. Even the smallest nurturing cage must therefore have a covering of wire screening so that as much of the UV light as possible will reach the lizards. As mentioned earlier, some shade must be provided.

First feeding

The time at which food is first taken can vary widely indeed. Whereas skinks take

Introduction to Lizard Breeding

their first food soon after birth, the reserves of some species can last for as long as a few weeks. You should not lose patience and resort to force-feeding; this in combination with the psychic stress will worsen the general health of the young lizard, thus endangering its chances of hardiness in the future. Food for young lizards must be rich in variety and prepared with utmost care, and the calcium and vitamin supply especially should not be neglected.

Live-Bearing Lizards

The form of reproduction that is described in the foregoing pages is called oviparity. This means that the development of the embryo takes place in the egg outside the mother's body. But in some lizards there occurs another type of reproduction, live-bearing ovoviviparous. In ovoviviparity, the embryo development takes place within the mother's body, albeit in a thin-skinned egg; therefore, for the most part, there is no connection to the circulation of the mother. There is also still another form of embryonic development, for example in some Australian skinks and in the desert night lizard, *Xantusia vigilis,* in whom the nourishment is partially supplied by the mother's metabolism. In the ovoviviparous lizards the young lizards hatch out of the egg membrane before, during, or immediately after the mother has laid the egg. Sometimes she eats the unfruitful egg right then. The mother does not nurture the freshly hatched lizards; on the contrary, very often they are in grave danger from the parent animals.

The live-born young animals should be raised in the terrarium in the same way as the incubator-hatched ones.

Sickness

The best way to prevent illness of your lizard pets is to take proper care of them. Even so, living space, climate, and nourishment of exotic lizards in the terrarium can never completely simulate the conditions of living free in the wild.

Note: Have the veterinarian do a fecal examination at one-year intervals for acclimated lizards. During the quarantine period have examinations three times at intervals of four weeks! Both internal illnesses and parasites can thus be recognized early and treatment begun.

Holding a large lizard. One person grasps the lizard so that the extermities are immobilized, to avoid being scratched by the sharp claws. A second person fixes the head and treats the lizard. The picture shows treatment of mouthrot.

Furthermore, you should always observe your lizards carefully. An ailment is usually evident in changed appearance and/or behavior.

As soon as you suspect illness, take the affected lizard to the veterinarian. Never experiment yourself! Unfortunately the treatment of reptiles is not generally part of veterinary practice. Nevertheless, since the veterinarian has experience in handling animals in general, he or she can show you how the treatment procedures should be carried out, medicines administered, or can, if necessary, prescribe. Surgical procedures and injections, obviously, should only be undertaken by the doctor. If he has never treated lizards, give him this chapter to read. All the described treatments have been successful at the Cologne Aquarium and Zoo.

Illness Diagnosed with the Naked Eye

Mites *(Ophionyssus)*
Symptoms: Gray-white feces of the parasites on the skin of the lizard, especially around the eye area. Mites themselves will often be seen later as barely pinhead sized, black, moving life forms. The parasites live on the blood of their host and prefer to bite the softer parts of the skin under the scales. Consequences: general weakness and stress from the constant itching. Perforations of the skin may lead to molting problems, and even, in the case of bad mite infestation, to skin necrosis and death (see page 49).
Treatment: If the mite infestation is already present at the time of purchase, bathe the lizard in its transport bag in a 0.2 percent Neguvon solution (0.04 ounces per quart [2 g/L]). The animal should then remain in the well-dampened bag (from which water is, however, evaporating) for several hours.

If mites appear on the animals in your terrarium, you must not only treat the lizards in

Sickness

the manner described above but the terrarium as well. Spray the cage and the decorations with a 0.2 percent solution of Neguvon. Use as fine a spray on the spray bottle as possible. Be particularly thorough, because mites often conceal themselves in the decorations. Treatment of both the lizards and the terrarium must be repeated after two weeks. You can also fight mites with a Vapona Insect Strip, which is hung in the terrarium. The Vapona strip is cut to deliver the correct amount of vapor as follows: ¼ inch (6.4 mm) of the narrow edge of the strip is cut for each 10 cubic feet (.28 m³) of cage volume. It is suspended from the top of the cage so that the lizard(s) cannot reach it. A hanger made from a bent paper clip works will for securing the strip to the roof of the cage. The strip is left in the terrarium for two to four days. Caution: (1) Do not handle the strip with your bare hands; use rubber or plastic gloves, or place your hand inside a plastic bag and dispose of your protective hand coverings after they have been in contact with the pest strip. A drawback to this method is that all food insects will be killed too. (2) Geckos with large skin wounds should not be treated with Neguvon because many species will not tolerate this preparation.

Ticks (Ixodidae Family)
Symptoms: Ticks bite the host animal, hold fast, and suck blood. The highly flattened arthropods, up to 0.12 inches (3 mm) in size, attach themselves firmly under the scales, preferring the soft skin parts between the shoulder and the hip joints.
Treatment: The parasites should not be pulled out because the mouth parts are usu-

ally left behind and can lead to infection. Treat with a 0.2 percent Neguvon solution as for mites (see page 46). If the lizard is very badly infested, Neguvon should not be used because the presence of many perforations of the skin makes poisoning a danger. In that case, lubricate the lizard with mineral oil. This treatment is lengthy and messy, so the animal must be kept in a quarantine terrarium while it is being treated. Hanging a Vapona Insect Strip can also help with a bad tick infestation.

External wounds
Symptoms: Bite wounds. Broken-off tail. Crushed toes.
Treatment: Care for a damp wound with antibiotic powder; if the edge becomes hard, apply antibiotic cream. Do not use adhesive tape or bandages. Wounded lizards should be kept in as sterile a terrarium as possible. Do not place an injured lizard in a sand or earth-filled terrarium because particles of soil may enter the moist open wounds.

Molting problems
Faults in maintenance, disturbance of general health, or an attack of external parasites can produce molting difficulties, as can vitamin deficiencies. Abnormally frequent shedding carries the danger of exhaustion; the cause may be an overadministration of vitamin preparations.
Treatment: Check the terrarium conditions, and especially the climate controls. Increase or decrease the vitamin dosage according to the problem.

Eyelid swelling
Vitamin A deficiency and/or infections of the eye or the area around the eyelids can result in eyelid swelling.

Treatment: If there are UV lights installed, check their intensity. Wash sticky eyes with sterile eyedrops. Instill 1 drop of sterile ophthalmic solution into the eye four times daily. Consult your veterinarian on the advisability of administering vitamin and/or antibiotic drops orally.

Convulsive trembling

Symptoms: In the early stages, only insignificant vibration is noticeable. In the middle stages, the limbs and the tail tremble if the lizard feels itself disturbed. This can be the case if you merely bump into the terrarium without actually injuring the animal. Don't confuse the cramping movements of the extremities with the "waving" of the agamas during courtship (see page 43). To be certain, take the animal in your hand. If the lizard is really suffering from convulsive trembling, you will feel the animal's body vibrating. In advanced convulsive trembling, the lizard lies flat on the ground, has long since refused nourishment, and when turned on its back just lies there, without being able to turn again. In such circumstances the lizard cannot, as a rule, be healed. Convulsive trembling is most often observed in iguanas.

Treatment: Administration of vitamin B is successful only if you use high doses and intervene in time. The veterinarian will inject thiamine hydrochloride intramuscularly, 25 to 100 mg per 2 pounds (25 to 100 mg/kg) of body weight, into the extremities daily for three to five days. During this time he can also alternate between the daily injection and the same dosage of thiamine tablets. After that, thiamine tablets, 100 mg per 2 pounds (100 mg/kg) of body weight, are alternated with a multivitamin preparation, 0.004 ounces per 2 pounds (1 ml/kg) of body weight, daily until complete disappearance of symptoms.

Metabolic Bone Disease

Insufficient deposit of calcium in the skeleton caused by too little calcium or vitamin D or too much phosphorus in the diet, too little UV irradiation; wastefully accelerated growth periods induced by excessively high temperatures can produce the illness. Usually not all the animals in a group display rachitic deficiencies; therefore it can be caused by disturbances in the particular lizard that is ailing.

Symptoms: Curvature or swelling of the spine, the limbs, and the tail, as well as deformities of the jaw. Appears most often in the growth phase.

Treatment: Check for the possible causes listed above. Massive administration of vitamin D is not advisable, because it is easy to overdose. A multivitamin preparation is helpful. Vionate, a supplement that is readily available and acceptable to most lizards, can be lightly dusted on fruit and vegetables before feeding them to herbivorous lizards. For lizards that are insectivorous, lightly dust on crickets or other feed insects.

Jaw suppuration, mouthrot

Following traumatic injury or chronic malnutrition, the mouth of some lizards may become inflamed and/or infected.

Symptoms: White to pinkish-gray patches, small hemorrhages, loose teeth, and sometimes a foul-smelling breath odor are characteristic. Affected lizards will refuse to feed and excessive mucus may be seen on the lips, which may be held slightly open.

Treatment: Disinfect with 3% hydrogen peroxide, then paint the affected tissue with full-strength Betadine Solution (do not use Betadine-Scrub). Often systemic antibiotics must be used. Ideally, your veterinarian should obtain a specimen of mucus or secretion from your lizard's mouth so that the exact type of bacteria and its sensitivity to specific antibiotics can be ascertained. Multivitamin drops may be of value, but you must not overdose them. All manipulations of the jaw must be performed with special care because a jaw weakened by chronic mouthrot may fracture and the lizard can no longer accept its usual nourishment by itself.

Skin necrosis

This ailment is usually caused by bacterial infections.

Symptoms: Abscesses (pus-filled places) in the skin.

Treatment: The veterinarian lances the abscess and disinfects the wound with 3 percent hydrogen peroxide solution. Antibiotic salve or powder is applied. If there is no improvement after a week, the antibiotic preparation must be changed. Food compounds must be checked to be sure they are of high quality. Make sure vitamin levels and UV lighting are sufficient and that the cage hygiene is adequate.

Pneumonia

Infection caused by bacteria, which is promoted by constantly overheating the terrarium and not lowering the temperature at night. Too cool a cage temperature also can stress lizards and make them more susceptible to infection.

Symptoms: Considerably decreased activity, bubbles at the nostrils, foamy mucus in the mouth, sneezing, not to be confused with sneezing of the iguana, which secretes salt from the nasal salt glands (see page 6), jerky opening and closing of the mouth, usually combined with rattling breath sounds.

Treatment: A six- to seven-day course of antibiotic or sulfa therapy. Terramycin, 6 to 10 mg per 2 pounds (6–10 mg/kg) of body weight by mouth divided into two doses per day for six days. Alternatively, Trimethroprim-sulfa at an intramuscular dose of 0.1 cc per 2 pounds (0.1 cc/kg) of the 24% suspension given daily for six days is usually effective. In addition a daily dose of multivitamins is recommended (see page 28). To avoid recurrence of the infection, the medication should be continued until five days after the complete disappearance of symptoms. If the medication does not prove successful during the specified time period, the microbes are resistant to the drug and the medication must be changed.

Inflammation of the intestinal tract

Symptoms: Considerably decreased activity, most of all decreased appetite. Runny, foul-smelling feces — though in monitor lizards this is normal — and, occasionally, a reddened cloaca.

Treatment: Through previous fecal examinations the possibility of worms and amoebic dysentery should be ruled out. If there has been no fecal examination, treatment must be begun at once because otherwise valuable time may be lost. Therapy is the same as for lung inflammation (see page 51).

Skin fungi

A variety of fungi, whose spread is promoted by unfavorable climatic conditions (mostly too low a temperature and too high a humidity), produce this illness.

Symptoms: Various large, flat skin changes without the development of pus.

Treatment: Difficult, since the fungus is already widespread in the deeper tissue layers before it becomes visible on the skin. Besides, many fungi are similar in appearance so that often the proper medication will not be found on the first attempt. Conofite is a fungicidal preparation that can be used with success on reptiles.

It may take about two weeks for any reaction to the medication to occur. Therefore do not change the medication any sooner.

Intestinal prolapse

Only rarely seen in lizards. The cause is not always clearly ascertainable. It is often induced by hard, dry feces, which are expelled with tremendous pushing. Intestinal parasites may also cause an intestinal prolapse.

Symptoms: Noticeable changes in the cloaca.

Treatment: If you discover the prolapse early enough, the veterinarian can usually, after careful cleansing with Betadine solution, massage the extruded portion of the intestine back again using antibiotic ointment or cream. An older prolapse, which has already begun to show inflammatory changes, will be massaged back with an antibiotic ointment or cream, which is applied daily. To give the unsettled intestine segment support, the cloaca is closed with a ball of cotton and taped with a small length of adhesive tape. The animal receives no food for two weeks so that the intestine will remain unstressed.

Hemipenis prolapse. If massaging back into place is not possible, the veterinarian must amputate.

Penis prolapse

A rare occurrence among lizards; its cause is not determined.

Symptoms: See drawing above.

Treatment: The extruded portion of the hemipenis is usually so badly swollen that it will no longer fit into the hemipenis sheath. The veterinarian can try to reduce the swelling by the application of anti-inflammatory ointment or cream and then to massage the hemipenis back. If this is not successful, amputation is necessary.

Egg-binding

The causes are not clearly established. Disturbances during the egg-laying process (see page 46) can have egg-laying trouble as a consequence.

Symptoms: Females with misshapen, swollen bodies. Eggs that can be clearly discerned as bumps in the body cavity or can be felt. (Though with geckos the eggs are always visible.) Futile pressing against previously dug holes.

Treatment: Injection with the labor-inducing drug oxytocin, 1.5 to 2.0 I.U. (international units) per 4 ounces (1.5–20 I.U./ 100gm) of body weight intramuscularly. If there is no improvement, the eggs must be removed by surgical intervention. Eggs that the lizard can't lay decay in the womb; the animal will die.

Sicknesses and Parasites Diagnosed by Fecal Examination or Section

Amoebic dysentery (Amebiasis)

This disease is caused by infection with a microbe (*Entamoeba invadens*). A lizard that has not been kept in quarantine long enough (see page 25) and then is placed in the terrarium can introduce the disease. Contagion is also possible through the keeper (hands, equipment and tools not disinfected — that is, by poor hygiene) or through escaped food insects. Moreover, if a terrarium is shared by turtles and lizards, spreading is possible because the lizards lick or eat feces or drink or bathe in turtle water. In turtles the amoebae usually do not cause disease unless the turtles are already stressed, but often these animals serve as vectors of this serious illness in lizards and snakes.

Symptoms: Amoebas are only evident in fresh feces or if a fecal examination and culture is undertaken. The presence of amoebas can also be confirmed after dissection of dead animals, since the disease alterations of the large intestine and the liver, particularly, are typical.

Treatment: If amoebic dysentery is diagnosed by fecal sample or surgical section, the sick lizard as well as all the other animals with which it has come into contact must be treated at once. The therapy is time-consuming, but at this time it is the only effective one; lizard deaths during the treatment are definitely caused by amoebic dysentery, rather than by the treatment itself. On the first day of treatment the prescription is metonidazol (Flagyl), 125 to 250 mg per 2 lb (125–250/kg) of body weight, administered orally; from the second to the sixth day, Terramycin, 6 to 10 mg per 2 lb (6–10 mg/kg) of body weight, orally on the seventh day, Flagyl, 125 to 250 mg per 2 lb (125–250 mg/kg) of body weight orally; from the eighth to the twelfth day, Terramycin, 6 to 10 mg per 2 lb (6–10 mg/kg) of body weight, orally; and on the thirteenth day wind up once again with Flagyl, 125 to 250 mg per 2 lb (125–250 mg/kg) of body weight, orally. Food should be withheld during the course of treatment to avoid stressing the intestinal tract. Also recommended are daily doses of multivitamins, 0.004 ounces per 2 pounds (1 ml/kg) of body weight. After conclusion of the treatment, lizards should be monitored with regular fecal examinations. Furthermore, lizards from an area of possible infection should not be placed in the company of other animals for at least six months after the end of the treatment.

Salmonella

Many fecal examinations will reveal signs of salmonella. They do not always harm the lizards but they can induce illness in the caretaker. Therefore you must always observe the best hygienic practices in handling the animals, in the use of equipment and tools, and in the cleaning of the terrarium.

Sickness

Worms

Worm eggs are in evidence in fecal examinations. Worms injure the host animals by depriving them of nourishment, by injury to the intestinal wall, and by the constipation that can be caused by the presence of large numbers. Especially dangerous for lizards is the constant reinfestation, which is possible with many types of worms. Because the lizards have only relatively small space at their disposal, the animals have frequent contact with their own feces and infect themselves anew. Terrarium animals can incur a massive infestation this way. The objection to worming that is frequently raised is that the medication for eradicating the worms can be toxic to the host animal. However, a lizard that is very badly infested with worms will soon die anyway without therapy. As soon as the worm eggs are detected in the feces, the affected lizard and all the other animals in the same terrarium must be treated.

Tapeworms damage the host not only by depriving it of nourishment but mainly by their suckers, hooks, and spines, which produce inflammation of the intestinal wall, especially during a severe infestation. Sections of tapeworm will frequently be found in the feces of infested animals.

Treatment: Droncit (praziquantel), 5 mg per 2 pounds (5 mg/kg); Panacur, 50 mg per 2 pounds (50 mg/kg) given orally for three consecutive days; Scolaban (bunamidine), 25 to 50 mg per 2 pounds (25 – 50 mg/kg); Telmintic (mebendazole), 20 mg per 2 pounds (20 mg/kg) for three consecutive days; or Vercom Paste (Febantel and praziquantel), 1 mg of praziquantel equivalent per 2 pounds (1 mg/kg) for three consecutive days.

Nematodes, roundworms appear very frequently and can often be seen in the feces.

Treatment: Pancur suspension 10 percent, 0.0012 to 0.002 ounces per 2 pounds (0.3 to 0.5 ml/kg) of body weight, administered orally. Repeat the treatment twice at intervals of about two weeks. The preparation has scarcely any side effects. Overdosage, particularly for that minority of lizards that weigh only a few grams, also has few serious consequences.

Maggots are more resistant than nematodes or roundworms.

Treatment: Maggots are best treated by first flushing open wounds with 3% hydrogen peroxide, then physically removing the fly maggots with a tweezer forceps. After the maggots have been removed, the wounds should be flushed again with hydrogen peroxide and then full-strength Betadine solution.

Visceral Gout

Deposits of uric acid salts, called urates, can occur in any organ, but most often develop in the kidneys, liver, and around the heart. These crystalline deposits irritate these

Lizards of the iguana family. Top left: spiny lizards (*Sceloporus malchitus*) Left: male, right: female; top right: spiny lizards (*Sceloporus jarrovi*); missle left: tropidurine lizards (*Tropidurus torquatus*); middle right: Mexican spiny lizards (*Sceloporus poinsetti*); bottom left: knight anole (*Anolis equestris*); bottom right: Catolina anole (*Anolis carolinensis*).

tissues and may cause the organ to fail entirely. Visceral gout occurs from three major sources: 1. the intake of excessive animal protein by normally herbivorous or nominally omnivorous lizards; 2. dehydration from imbibing insufficient water (or other source of moisture from the food); 3. some antibiotics can damage the kidneys suffi-ciently to reduce their ability to clear waste products.

Symptoms: Jerky opening and closing of the mouth as with lung inflammation (see page 49) but without the bubbling at the nostrils. Apathy.

Treatment: Unfortunately there is no effective treatment possible at this time.

Large lizards. Top left: Tegu (*Tubinambis teguixin nigropunctatus*) with the egg of another anaimal). It will be broken and its contents licked out. Top right: Nile monitor (*Varanus niloticus*); **bottom: Cape monitor (***Varanus exanthmaticus*)—monitors also like to eat eggs of birds and reptiles.

Plants in the Terrarium

Terrarium plants do not only perform a decorative function. They also influence the microclimate, provide the lizards with cover, and create a visual screen, thus establishing the territories that are necessary for many types of lizards.

Important note: Some of the plants described have juices that can be injurious to health if they come into contact with the skin or mucous membranes of humans. After work with plants, wash your hands thoroughly, rinse away any juices from leaves or stems that have sprayed onto your face, and *never* put any portion of a plant into your mouth. Warn children about this!

Location of the Planted Terrarium

Light is necessary for plant life. It is essential for the production of chlorophyll, which in turn is a requirement for plant vigor. If there is too little light available, the plant will try to grow toward it. It produces longer and thinner shoots with pale little leaves, and the plant yellows. The plant can only compensate in this fashion for a very short time, because not enough chlorophyll is being created; the plant is "starving" in spite of the nutrient-rich soil.

You must therefore choose the brightest possible location for a planted terrarium. If some of the plants continue to show signs of lack of light, they should be removed from the terrarium and placed in a very bright spot or on a balcony for a while.

Planting Medium

The planting medium for terrarium plants is leafmold or decayed pine needles. If the depth is greater than 0.2 inches (5 cm), provide a drainage layer of gravel or broken flower pots. Then the water can trickle through the dry earth and collect in the pebble or crockery layer. A floor of heavy clay or humus becomes waterlogged easily and in dry periods will become hard and cracked.

Many terrarium plants grow as epiphytes, or air plants; they are planted as follows: Free the root ball of the dry soil, pack it into sphagnum moss, coconut fiber, fern roots, or other plant material that drains readily, and press it into the fork of an epiphyte support or tie or nail it to a branch. Air plants can also be stuck in a suitably large hole in a branch or a crack. Wherever you put it, the water must be able to drain off easily; epiphytes have adapted to this way of living to avoid standing water.

Opuntia   *Aloe variegate*

Sansevieria trifasciata   *Echeveria*
(bowstring hemp)

Plants for desert terrarium.

Plants in the Terrarium

Watering

For watering use only clean rainwater or salt-free water that you can buy or produce yourself with an ion-exchanger (pet store). The use of salt-free water is essential for the culture of Tillandsia and other bromeliads with scaly leaves (see page 58). The silver-white scales of the bromeliads function to take up moisture and nutrients. If they are encrusted with salts they can no longer do so. When salt-free water is used, such deposits do not build up on the leaves of the terrarium plants.

Plant Pests

No sprays or insecticides should be used in the terrarium! Try to wipe away leaf aphids, woolly apple aphids, and scale with a soft, damp cloth or a sponge. And increase the humidity, since these insects thrive in a setting that is too dry. If the noxious insects are still tenacious, there is nothing to do but remove the affected plants from the terrarium. Now you can use an insecticide. Afterwards wait at least two, and better four weeks before replacing them in the terrarium, and keep rinsing them off! If you continue having repeated attacks of pests, the only sure remedy is to change to another kind of plant.

Changing Plants

Plants that get too little light or are attacked by insects must be removed from the terrarium. You'll make the removal easier if you leave the plants in pots and sink them into the floor material deeply enough so that the tops are no longer visible. You should also transfer a plant if it needs cutting back or if the new shoots are in danger from the lizards.

Tip: If you want to use the occasion of the removal to fertilize, use bone meal or dehydrated manure according to the directions on the package.

Choosing Plants

It isn't necessary for the lizards' well-being that the plants come from the same area that they do. But many terrarium enthusiasts find it fun to create geographical unity between animals and planting. For this rea-

Scindapsus aureus (pothos)

Ficus pumila

Vriesia splendens

Maranta leuconeura

Plants for the rain-forest terrarium.

Plants in the Terrarium

son, this discussion of plants is arranged according to their range of distribution. If you would like to know more about terrarium plants, you can read about them in the literature (see Books for Further Help, page 85).

Make sure when you buy terrarium plants that they are strong enough for your lizards. Will they survive a leap, for instance, or tightly clinging sharp claws? Please read the advice in the plant descriptions (below). It generally holds true that hard-leaved, dark green plants are less delicate than tender-leaved, bright green or even colored-leaved types. In choosing terrarium plants, always consider the effects of the heat, lighting, and UV lamps.

Plants from North, Central, and South America

Rain-forest plants

Of the multitude of plants from the tropical rain forests of Central and South America, there is a wide choice wonderfully suited for terrariums available at plant stores and nurseries. So it's easy to find the right ones for any terrarium and also for any taste and pocketbook.

Dieffenbachia (*Dieffenbachia*), available in many varieties and forms of culture. Ground plants: only suitable as young plants or for large terrariums with quiet inhabitants; leaves tear easily. The "gold-dust" plant, *Dieffenbachia,* is toxic to humans and animals.

Philodendrons (*Philodendron*) available in many species.

Philodendron panduriforme, hanging and climbing plants with medium-large leaves.

Like many other species and culture forms of this family, they put out air roots, which branch decoratively in water and no longer need soil.

Philodendron martianum, firm, decorative single plants; needs a great deal of light.

Philodendron scandens, suitable ground, hanging, or climbing plants. Since leaves are small and firm, can be used for free-standing plantings; easy to increase by cuttings (cutting outer ends of plant).

Spathyphyllum (*Spathyphyllum*), the smaller forms are well suited to the terrarium. Ground plants; occasionally with white blooms.

Syngonium (*Syngonium*), offered in many varieties and forms. Climbing plants with leaves somewhat similar to philodendron.

Bromeliads (*Bromeliaceae*), because of their typical growth habits and their usually epiphytical life style, are best for creating small uncluttered landscapes.

Vriesia splendens, a large variety with beautifully marked leaves, but there are forms available that remain small. Epiphytic; leaves grow in the form of a rosette, as do those of most ananas, forming a well in which water collects; thus these plants secure their water and nourishment needs and the wells serve many lizards as drinking places.

Vriesia psittacina, small variety; epiphytic; sensitive to standing water.

Tillandsia, available in many varieties. Model example of epiphytic habit; grows partly without soil, only bound to wood; needs much light and high humidity at night.

Guzmania, many varieties and hybrids available. Various sizes, therefore suitable for many terrariums; epiphytic; sensitive to standing water.

Plants in the Terrarium

Cryptanthus, available in many varieties. Very decorative; grows mainly on the ground and only occasionally epiphytically. When growing on the ground it will not tolerate standing water; shoots are easily broken off by the animals, so propagation must be done outside the terrarium.

Nidularium, many varieties and hybrids offered; epiphytic; most rather large but without problems.

Aechmea fasciata, Aechmea chantinii, Aechmea fulgens, large, epiphytic-growing ananas; suitable for larger terrariums only.

Billbergia, a number of varieties sometimes available; epiphytic; firm; freely blooming.

Spiderwort (*Tradescantia*), available in many varieties and forms; ground, hanging, and climbing plants; easy to propagate through cuttings (cutting outer ends of plant).

Marantas (*Maranta leuconeura, Calathea makoyana, Calathea ornata*), ground plants; except for the first-mentioned variety, suitable only for larger terrariums; needs light.

Peperomia (*Peperomia*), available in many varieties and forms. Ground plants; some varieties epiphytic; avoid standing water because roots rot quickly. Only suitable for light, not very active lizards.

Phlebodium (*Polypodium aureum*), epiphytically growing fern for larger terrariums.

Desert plants

The maintenance of plants from dry areas often turns out to be difficult because the humidity and light conditions in the terrarium are usually inadequate for them. If you install the proper lighting fixtures, the humidity then drops even more. Plants that need dryness must therefore be changed more often so that they can recover.

Agave (*Agave*), few varieties available; varieties with contained growth habits well suited for the terrarium.

Dyckia (*Dyckia*), few varieties and seldom available; nonepiphytic anana.

Hechtia (*Hechtia*), few varieties and seldom available; nonepiphytic anana.

Columnar cactus (*Cereus*), a number of varieties available; only suitable for high terrariums; avoid varieties with especially large thorns.

Opuntia (*Opuntia*), many varieties available; grows to various sizes; avoid varieties with especially large thorns.

Echeveria (*Echeveria*), many varieties available; water carefully because roots rot easily.

Plants from Southeast Asia

Rain-forest plants

A number of commercially available decorative plants are suitable for planting in a terrarium in which lizards from Southeast Asia will be kept.

Aglaonema (*Aglaonema*), available in many varieties and forms. Ground plants, must be cut back from time to time so that leafy branches will put forth underneath; can be propagated by cuttings (cutting off outer ends).

Pothos (*Scindapsus aureus*), ground, hanging, and climbing plants; thrives under various adverse conditions. With sufficient humidity produces air roots that branch out in water and then no longer need soil; easy to propagate by cutting.

Ficus (*Ficus benjamina*), small-leaved ornamental fig; suitable for large terrariums only. Cut back if crown broadens under the terrarium roof and shuts out too much light.

Plants in the Terrarium

Ficus (*Ficus pumila*), ground, hanging, and climbing plants; thrives best on damp walls; damaged by standing water.

Sword fern (*Nephrolepsis exaltata*), available in many forms. Ground plants; avoid standing water and floor heat.

Staghorn fern (*Platycerium grande*), typical epiphyte, only suitable for the large terrarium; outer leaves must be free-standing; root ball should not dry out.

Ginger (*Zingiber officinale*), ground plant, well suited to background planting.

Desert plants

The choice of plants for an Asiatic desert terrarium is very small.

Sedum (*Sedum*), many varieties from many different habitats available; can be maintained at a variety of temperatures.

Plants from Africa

Rain-forest plants

Nurseries offer few plants from the tropical rain forests of Africa and Madagascar.

Dracena (*Dracaena deremensis*), ground plants that quickly grow to large size; must be cut back from time to time; cuttings develop roots easily.

Dracena (*Dracaena sanderiana, Dracaena godseffiana*), ground plants, more difficult to raise than *Dracaena deremensis; Dracaena godseffiana,* with tender leaves, only suitable for quiet lizards.

Anubias (*Anubias*), a few varieties offered from time to time as aquarium plants; also grows in swampy ground.

Stephanotis (*Stephanotis floribunda*), ground plants, which under favorable conditions will climb up the lizards' climbing branches; blooms occasionally; suitable for small Phelsuma species (see page 36).

Asparagus fern (*Asparagus falcatus*), ground plants; injured by standing water; shoots are supported by branches growing in the same direction.

Asparagus fern (*Asparagus densiflorus*), hanging plant; provide good drainage.

Chlorophytum (*Chlorophytum comosum*), ground and hanging plants; must not be kept too warm.

Desert plants

Many plants from African dry areas south of the Sahara are popular houseplants and on that account are often available from nurseries.

Bowstring hemp (*Sansevieria trifasciata*), available in various large forms; must be watered more often than crassulas.

Jade plants (*Crassula falcata, Crassula portulacea*), should be changed frequently because the new shoots develop quickly.

Wolf's milk, Spurge (*Euphorbia*), many varieties and various sizes available; many can be propagated by cuttings of side shoots; the "milk" that is exuded can be dried up with charcoal powder and the cutting planted a few days later. This plant family is toxic to humans and most animals. Many humans are extremely sensitive to the very presence of these plants in their households.

Aloe (*Aloe arborescens*), large growing, almost bush variety; especially well suited for large terrariums.

Aloe (*Aloe variegata*), considerably smaller than *Aloe arborescens;* has no thorns; especially suitable for small lizards.

Plants in the Terrarium

Gasteria (*Gasteria*), some varieties available from time to time; uncomplicated maintenance.

Haworthia (*Haworthia*), some varieties available from time to time; well suited to small terrariums.

Plants from Australia

Rain-forest plants

Only a few plants and lizards from Australia and the islands of the Pacific that are suitable for keeping the terrarium are available to us.

Ficus (*Ficus rubiginosa*), ground plants; only the young plants are suitable for use in large terrariums; injured by standing water.

Screw-pine (*Pandanus veitchii*), ground plants; as young plants, suitable for large terrariums. Care is necessary in handling as there are sharp thorns around the edges of the leaves.

Blechnum (*Blechnum gibbum*), ground plants; injured by standing water but the root ball should never dry out.

Staghorn fern (*Platycerium alcicorne*), typical epiphyte; only suitable for large terrariums; outer leaves must be free-standing; root ball should not dry out.

Desert plants

Only a few species of plants from the thin savannah-woods of Australia are suitable for transplanting into the terrarium.

False aralia (*Dizygotheca elegantissima*), ground plants for the large terrarium; not suitable for climbing lizards.

Silk oak (*Grevillea robusta*), ground plants for the large terrarium; injured by standing water; not suitable for climbing lizards.

Kangaroo vine (*Cissus antarctica*), ground, hanging, and climbing plants for a bright location.

Plants from the Islands of the Western Mediterranean

Plants from this environment are easy to get but cannot be kept over the summer, especially in a small terrarium. Only during the winter months, when temperatures are lower, will these plants from the islands of the western Mediterranean thrive in the terrarium.

Oleander, rose bay (*Nerium oleander*), offered in a number of forms. Ground plants, must be cut back from time to time; only suited to large terrariums. Oleander is extremely toxic to humans and almost all animals.

English ivy (*Hedera helix*), hard ground and climbing plant; colored leaved forms more sensitive than green ones. English ivy is toxic to most animals when eaten.

Sedum (*Sedum*), available in many varieties; not all originated in the Mediterranean area and the Canary Islands.

House leek (*Sempervivum*), many kinds available; ground plants.

Rosemary (*Rosmarinus officinalis*), ground plants; similar to myrtle but dainty and thus suitable for small terrariums; cut back long shoots.

Butcher's broom (*Ruscus aculeatus*), is offered occasionally; ground plants; need loamy soil enriched with humus.

Myrtle (*Myrtus communis*), various sizes available; ground plants; cut back long shoots.

Canary Islands date palm (*Phoenix canariensis*), ground plants; suitable for large terrariums; water moderately but regularly.

Setting Up Desert, Rain-Forest, and Water Terrariums

The length measurements given are maximums for full-grown animals; these sizes are almost never reached in a terrarium. The head-torso length is measured from the snout to the cloacal vent. The terrarium measurements describe length by width by height and are suitable — unless otherwise specified — for adult animals. These terrarium measurements are derived from many years of experience.

Important note: Reptiles that are covered by the Washington Convention on International Trade in Endangered Species (WA) are identified by the symbol * (see Endangered Species Regulations, page 24). The name of the biologist who identified each species is given, with the date of his work, immediately after the Latin binomial designation.

Warning: While handling reptiles, the keeper must reckon with wounds produced by bites, tail blows, or scratches. Even very small wounds must be seen by a doctor at once. Only a doctor can treat them properly.

Order: Crocodiles (Crocodylia)
Family: Alligators (Alligatoridae)

The alligators and the caimans, are different from the crocodiles in that when the mouth is closed, the teeth of the lower jaw are not visible. The are covered by the upper jaw and there is a groove provided in the upper jaw for the large fourth tooth of the lower jaw. It does happen, though, that alligators and caimans that have not bred true to type do exhibit jaw deformities with the teeth disposed to the outside.

All Alligatoridae are severely endangered by the hunt for skins for the leather industry and therefore are protected by the Washington Endangered Species Agreement (see page 24). Of the whole family of alligators, only the dwarf caiman is a candidate for keeping in a terrarium. Though not a lizard, it is included because it may be of interest to some hobbyists.

Differences between sexes: Among Alligatoridae raised together, as a rule, the male animals are larger than the females and their skull is bigger. Among lizards that have not been raised together differentiations between the sexes on the basis of these elements is scarcely possible because they depend on so many factors. Definite determination that the animal in question is male can only be established by palpation of the penis (see page 41). For this the dwarf caiman must have attained a body length of at least 32 inches (80 cm).

Reproduction: Reproduction of the dwarf caiman takes place in the months between December and April. During this time the male gives out threatening gutteral sounds. Mating takes place at night. Before egg-laying — in the months from May to August — the female builds a nest from plant stems, leaves, and similar material. The warmth given off by the decaying nest materials incubates the eggs. When kept in a terrarium, the caiman lays her eggs in a sand pit, too; the hard-shelled eggs must then be transferred to an incubator (see page 43). The maturation time is 100 to 115 days at 82° to 86°F (28 to 30°C).

Smaller lizards. Top left: southern alligator lizards *(Gerrhonotus multicarinatus)*; top right: Canary Island lizard *(Gallotia galloti)*; bottom: pityuses lizard *(Podarcis pityusensis)*.

Setting up Desert, Rain-Forest, and Water Terrariums

Dwarf caiman*
Photograph on back cover
Paleosuchus palpebrosus (Cuvier, 1807)
Endangered species regulation: WA II C2
Total length: 56 inches (140 cm). *Head-torso length:* 28 inches (70 cm).
Distribution and Description: Northern South America, southward to latitude 20. *Habitat:* Shallows, but also to some extent fast-moving water, even areas of rapids. *Identifying characteristics:* Iris chestnut brown, upper eyelid hardened, no ridge between the eyes. *Behavior:* Solitary without notable territorial behavior. Definitely recognizes different people and connects specific experiences with them.
Maintenance: Shallow-water terrarium, with a land portion as a shelf. The terrarium size will change because the space requirements increase with growth. For three caimans in the first year (total length to 20 inches [50 cm]): 28 × 28 × 20 inches (70 × 70 × 50 cm); water depth 2 inches (5 cm). Second to fourth year (total length to 30 inches [75 cm]): 48 × 36 × 20 inches (120 × 90 × 50 cm), water depth 4 inches (10 cm). Fifth to seventh year (total length to 40 inches [100 cm]): 60 × 44 × 28 inches (150 × 110 × 70 cm) water depth 6 inches (15 cm). For a breeding pair: 80 × 80 × 40 inches (200 × 200 × 100 cm), water depth of 20 inches (50 cm). Only when there are hanging epiphytes should terrariums be higher than specified.
Decorations: Stones, stumps, epiphytic plants from the rain forests of Central and South America (see page 58). For breeding, plant material for nest building.
Temperature: Day and night, 77° to 86°F (25–30°C); *Water:* 77°F (25°C).
Humidity: 70 to 90 percent.
Food: About a fifth of a mouse or a rat, otherwise freshwater fish. In the wild, young animals also eat snails and freshwater shrimp.

Order: Scaly Reptiles (Squamata) Family: Gecko (Gekkonidae)

Almost all the members of this family have adhesive lamellae on the undersides of their toes (see page 5); the leopard gecko (page 7) is one of the few exceptions. Geckos pay special attention to the toes during molting. The hook cells of the lamellae are unable to function because of the residue of old skin, so the geckos can no longer climb as they are accustomed to. You as caretaker must be sure that no old skin is left on the toes during molting. (Rule out the possibilities for emergencies.) Molting problems result from too low a humidity and as a consequence of metabolic disturbances. Many geckos will accept fruit nectar or fruit puree;

Skinks. Top left: spiny-tailed skink (*Egernia cunninghami*); top right: blue-tongued skink (*Tilqua gigas*); middle left: five-lined skink (*Eumeces fasciatus*), juvenile; middle right: *Mabuya quinquetaeniata*; bottom left: Gerrard's blue-tongued skink (*Tilqua gerrardii*), unusually colored juvenile; bottom right: Gerrard's blue-tongued skink (*Tilqua gerrardii*), old animal, easy to recognize by its massive skull.

Setting up Desert, Rain-Forest, and Water Terrariums

a *small* amount of multivitamin-mineral supplement can be added to these food items to enhance the overall nutrition of these lizards.

Almost all species of the genus *Phelsuma* are named in WA II C2. Fortunately, however, many survive in terrariums.

Differences between the sexes: All gecko males differ from the females in having a shorter, broader head, preanal pores, and the sheaths with the hemipenies (see page 41).

Reproduction: Geckos lay as many as two hard-shelled eggs up to three times a year, mostly on wood. They are especially fond of places where bark is missing from a trunk or woody plant fibers are lying on top of each other, for example on a palm trunk. These eggs must be transferred to the incubator (see page 43) wood and all so that none of them will be lost. The exception is the leopard gecko, which lays its soft-shelled eggs on the damp floor of its hole. The maturation time in the incubator is about 45 to 60 days at 79° to 90°F (26°–32°C). It is advisable to use the lower temperature for a longer maturation period. The young are then hardier and grow more quickly than lizards matured at the higher temperature. The sex of leopard geckos is influenced by the temperature at which their eggs are incubated.

Social behavior: Almost all geckos live in loose groups. Every animal has its own defined territory but also needs the nearness of other geckos, which it greets on the border, threatens, or courts. The caretaker can easily observe this lively communication.

General advice for maintenance: If a gecko must be caught, the animal should be grasped carefully but firmly by the torso and held fast. *Caution:* Never grasp the tail, because the gecko may cast it off (see page 5). As soon as you have caught a gecko, it will try to turn in your hand, which — especially with Madagascar geckos — may quickly lead to skin injury. A firm grip will hinder this. If, in spite of all caution, the skin does tear, it must be smoothed and spread back with gentle pressure. Usually after a few days it will have grown back again and only a small "seam" remain.

Warning: If you must handle a tokay in the terrarium, be particularly careful and grasp it firmly if you want to catch it. The tokay can bite. Once it has bitten, it holds on tight. The mouth can only be opened with a lever; or you can hold the tokay under water until the animal lets go.

Asiatic house gecko
Photograph page 36
Hemidactylus frenatus
(Duméril and Bibron, 1836)
Total length: 6 inches (15 cm). *Head-torso length:* 3 inches (7 cm).
Distribution and Description: Originally Southeast Asia, but subsequently it has spread to almost all tropical continents. *Habitat:* Woods, thickets, cultivated land, human settlements. *Identifying characteristics:* Slit pupil. Adhesive lamellae do not reach to tips of toes, so the genus is also called the "half-finger gecko." *Behavior:* Nocturnal. Lives in loose groups.
Maintenance: High terrarium, 12 × 12 × 16 inches (30 × 30 × 40 cm) for one male and two females. *Decoration:* Branches and bark in the background; they must be removable because eggs will be attached and portions of the decorations must be easy to transfer to the incubator. Plants are not absolutely neces-

Setting up Desert, Rain-Forest, and Water Terrariums

sary. *Temperature:* By day 73° to 86°F (23–30°C); by night 68° to 77° (20–25°C). *Humidity:* 70 to 90 percent. *Food:* Insects, spiders, baby mice. Drinking water will be licked from the decorations or from flat saucers.

Striped Madagascar gecko ∗
Phelsuma lineata (Gray, 1842)
Endangered species designation: WA II C2
Total length: 5 inches (12 cm). *Head-torso length:* 2 inches (6 cm).
Distribution and Description: Madagascar. *Habitat:* Woods, bush country, cultivated land. *Identifying characteristics:* No slit pupil. Adhesive lamellae. *Behavior:* Diurnal. Lives on trees and leaves. Lives in loose groups.
Maintenance: High terrarium, 12 × 12 × 16 inches (30 × 30 × 40 cm) for one male and 1 female; for every additional animal add 2 inches (5 cm) more to each measurement. *Decoration:* Branches and a number of plants from Africa and Madagascar (see page 60). Sunning places and UV lighting. *Temperature:* By day 79° to 86°F (26–30°C); by night 64° to 73°F (18–23° C). *Humidity:* 60 to 80 percent. *Food:* Insects, spiders, fruit nectar or puree. Drinking water will be licked from plants; spray them with water once daily.

Gold dust Madagascar day geckos
Phelsuma laticauda (Boettger, 1880)
Photographs on page 36 and back cover
Endangered species designation:
WA II C2
Total length: 5 inches (12 cm). *Head-torso length:* 2 inches (6 cm).

Distribution and Description: Eastern Madagascar, Nossi Bé, Comoro Islands. *Habitat:* Woods, bush country, cultivated lands. *Identifying characteristics:* Pupils without slits. Adhesive lamellae. *Behavior:* Diurnal. Lives on trees and leaves. Lives in loose groups.
Maintenance: High terrarium, 12 × 12 × 16 inches (30 × 30 × 40 cm) for one male and one female; for each additional animal add 2 inches (5 cm) to each measurement. *Decorations:* Branches and a variety of plants from Africa and Madagascar (see page 60). Sunning places UV lighting. *Temperature:* By day 79° to 86°F (26–30°C); by night 64° to 73°F (18–23°C). *Humidity:* 50 to 70 percent. *Food:* Insects and spiders; fruit nectar or puree. Drinking water is licked from plants; spray them with water once daily.

Large Madagascar geckos
Photograph page 38
Phelsuma madagascariensis (Gray, 1831)
Endangered species designation:
WA II C2
Total length: 10 inches (25 cm). *Head-torso length:* 5 inches (13 cm).
Distribution and Description: In numerous subspecies on Madagascar, Nossi Bé, and other small neighboring islands and on some of the Seychelles. *Habitat:* Woods, bush country, cultivated land. *Identifying characteristics:* No slit pupil. Adhesive lamellae. *Behavior:* Diurnal. Lives in trees and on leaves. Lives in loose groups.
Maintenance: Terrarium, 24 × 16 × 16 inches (60 × 40 × 40 cm) for one male and one female. More animals should only be kept together in a very large terrarium or in a greenhouse. *Decoration:* Branches and

Setting up Desert, Rain-Forest, and Water Terrariums

plenty of plants from Africa and Madagascar (see page 60). Sunning places and UV lighting. *Temperature:* By day, 79° to 86°F (26–30°C); by night 64° to 73°F (18–23°C). *Humidity:* 60 to 80 percent. *Food:* Insects and spiders; fruit nectar or puree. Drinking water will be licked from the plants; spray them with water once daily.

Tokay gecko
Photograph on page 38 and back cover
Gecko gecko (Linnaeus, 1758)
Total length: 14 inches (356 cm). *Head-torso length:* 7 inches (17 cm).
Distribution and Description: From northeast India across Indochina eastward to western New Guinea. *Habitat:* Rain forests, human settlements. *Identifying characteristics:* Slit pupil. Adhesive lamellae. *Behavior:* Nocturnal. Lives on trees, also on beams of houses. Solitary. Calls loudly and resoundingly in the evening hours "to-kay, to-kay."
Maintenance: Cube-shaped terrarium, 16 × 16 × 16 inches (40 × 40 × 40 cm) for one animal. If you want to have several (all the same species), you need a terrarium 32 × 16 × 16 inches (80 × 40 × 40 cm) with sliding separators or gates. *Decoration:* Branches and bark in the background so that eggs can be transferred to the incubator without difficulty. Plants are not absolutely necessary. *Temperature:* By day 77° to 86°F (25–30°C); by night 68° to 77°F (20–25°C). *Humidity:* 70 to 90 percent. *Food:* Large insects, baby mice, and rats. In the natural habitat reptiles and bird nestlings also. Drinking water will be licked from the decorations or from shallow saucers; spray plants with water once daily.

Leopard gecko
Photograph 38
Eublepharis macularis (Blyth, 1854)
Total length: 8 inches (20 cm). *Head-torso length:* 5 inches (12 cm).
Distribution and Description: Asia Minor to northwestern India. *Habitat:* Dry areas. *Identifying characteristics:* Slit pupils; movable eyelid. No adhesive lamellae but claws. Juveniles are still unspotted, with broad, dark-brown horizontal stripes. *Behavior:* Nocturnal. Spends days in cool holes. Ground dwelling. Lives in loose groups; holes are inhabited commonly.
Maintenance: Shallow terrarium, 20 × 20 × 16 inches (50 × 50 × 40 cm) for one male and two females; for every additional animal add 2 inches (5 cm) more to length and width. *Decoration:* Stones, sand, gravel. Caves, which should be kept moderately damp. *Temperature:* By day 86°F (30°C); by night 68°F (20°C). Pseudo-winter rest from November to February: constant 68°F (20°C; heat lamp not turned on). *Humidity:* 50 to 70 percent. *Food:* Insects, spiders, baby mice. Drinking water will be licked from the decorations or from shallow saucers; spray plants with water once daily.

Family: Iguana (Iguanidae)

Most iguanas have helmets, or casques — flaps of skin or crests on the head, back, tail, or throat. Such features are mostly seen in males only. If they do occur in both sexes, the ones in females are always less striking than those of males. All anoles have an erectile dewlap (see drawing on page **44**). The females of this species also have a dewlap,

Setting up Desert, Rain-Forest, and Water Terrariums

but it is always smaller and less brilliant in color than that of the male. During the delineation and defense of their territories, during courtship, and during threatening, the dewlap is erected and presented with vigorous head nodding. In some species there are neck and back crests, which are inflated and displayed in excitement. The erecting and flattening of the torso also belongs to the body language of the iguanas.

Like the geckos, all the anole species have adhesive lamellae on the undersides of their toes (see page 5), by means of which they can even run along a plate of glass. Therefore you need to be particularly careful when working in the terrarium.

On the basis of marking studies of free-living anoles, it has been determined that the lizards of this genus do not become very old. The reason for this lies in their enormous activity. Because anoles are so very busy about their own affairs, they often fail to notice predators. In the studied population, the majority of the marked lizards were no longer to be seen after two years. Considerably older — up to fifteen years — were the larger and less temperamental kinds like the common iguana.

Differences between the sexes: Male basilisks are easy to tell from the females because of their skin flaps and crests. Among the common iguanas both sexes have crests. A grown male of this species is recognizable by its larger skull and the mostly yellow-orange color of its limbs. Spiny iguanas have femoral pores (see page 41), which are more prominent in the male than in the female. The male of the tropidurine lizards has a black spot on its throat, which is missing in the female. In anole males there are two noticeably larger scales behind the cloaca; females of this species do not have enlarged scales. In the mature males of all the species named, recognizable sheaths containing the hemipenies (see page 42) can be seen at the root of the tail. The sex of the younger lizards can only be determined with a probe (see page 42).

Reproduction: Some spiny lizard species are ovoviviparous (see page 45), but all other iguanids bury their eggs in holes of various shapes. The number of eggs varies according to species and range from two to forty. The clutch of eggs must be transferred to an incubator. Only thus can the young animals that hatch later be protected from the usually cannibalistic adult animals. Though the ovoviviparously born spiny lizards are somewhat protected by a differently colored skin, successful breeding nevertheless depends on caring for them separately.

General advice for maintenance: In suitably large terrariums with well-constructed decorations, two or more males of the genera *Sceloporus, Tropidurus,* and *Anolis* — except for *Anolis equestris* — can be kept together. Most male common iguanas and basilisks of the same species cannot be kept in one terrarium, however. Besides the physical stress, the psychological stress is too great for the lower-ranked animal and will end in death. But keeping different species in one terrarium is possible.

Basilisks, especially, act extremely frightened during the initial period of being kept in a terrarium. They jump against the glass, which is invisible to them, and injure their snouts. Therefore you should provide extensive cover with suitable decoration or cover the quarantine terrarium.

Setting up Desert, Rain-Forest, and Water Terrariums

Iguanas and basilisks love to bathe, so a water bath is essential. In length it should be at least one and a half times the head-torso length of the largest lizard and in width once the head-torso length. Most feces are dropped during swimming, so the water must be changed frequently. Daily water change will be easy if you install a direct water line and drainage system.

Note: The following spiny lizards have no distinguishing English names.

Spiny lizards
Photograph page 53
Sceloporus poinsetti
(Baird and Girard, 1852)
Total length: 10 inches (26 cm). *Head-torso length:* 5 inches (12 cm).
Distribution and Description: From southwestern North America (Texas and New Mexico) southward to central Mexico. *Habitat:* In mountains to 8,200 feet (2,500 m); hot, dry, stony slopes. *Identifying characteristics:* Scales that are "keeled," that is to say, ending in sharp points, spiny. *Behavior:* Diurnal. Ground-dwelling. Lives in small groups; dominant males live in privileged areas. Ovoviviparous. Young animals should be separated from cannibalistic parent animals.
Maintenance: Terrarium 60 × 24 × 24 inches (150 × 60 × 60 cm) for two males and four females. *Decoration:* Stones, pebbles, sand. Sunning spots and UV lighting. Sun terrarium. *Temperature:* By day 104°F (40°C) exactly but the animals must be able to crawl into cooler areas; by night 59°F (15°C). Pseudo-winter rest from November to February at 59° to 68°F (15–20°C; reflector lamp not turned on). *Humidity:* 50 to 70 percent. *Food:* Insects, spiders, baby mice, also occasionally leaves and flowers. Drinking water will be licked from the decorations or from shallow saucers; spray plants with water once daily.

Spiny lizard
Photograph page 53
Sceloporus jarrovi (Cope, 1875)
Total length: 7 inches (17 cm). *Head-torso length:* 3 inches (7 cm).
Distribution and Description: From southwestern North America (Arizona, New Mexico) southward to southern Mexico. *Habitat:* Mountains from 4,900 to 9,800 feet (1,500 to 3,000 m), especially somewhat damp regions. *Identifying characteristics:* Scales keeled. *Behavior:* Diurnal. Ground-dwelling. Lives in small groups, dominant males on display spots. Ovoviviparous. Young animals must be separated from the cannibalistic parents.
Maintenance: Terrarium, 60 × 24 × 24 inches (150 × 60 × 60 cm) for two males and four females. *Decoration:* Stones, stumps, sand or sandy soil, not completely dry. Plants from the dry areas of North and Central America (see page 58). Sunning places and UV lighting. Sun terrarium. *Temperature:* By day exactly 95°F (35°C), and the animals must be able to crawl into cooler areas; by night 59°F (15°C). From November to February pseudo-winter rest at 59° to 68°F (15–20°C; reflector lamp not turned on). *Humidity:* 50 to 70 percent. *Food:* Insects, spiders, baby mice, also occasionally leaves and flowers. Drinking water will be licked from the decorations or from shallow saucers; spray plants with water once daily.

Setting up Desert, Rain-Forest, and Water Terrariums

Spiny lizards
Photograph on page 53
Sceloporus malachitus (Cope, 1864)
Total length: 8 inches (20 cm). *Head-torso length:* 4 inches (7 cm)
Distribution and Description: Central America (Mexico, Panama). *Habitat:* Mountains 4,900 feet (1,500 m); light woods. *Identifying characteristics:* Scales keeled. *Behavior:* Diurnal. Inhabits ground and tree trunks. Lives in small groups, dominant males on display spots. Ovoviviparous. Young animals must be kept separated from the cannibalistic parents.
Maintenance: Terrarium 60 × 24 × 24 inches (150 × 60 × 60 cm) for two males and four females. *Decoration:* Stones, stumps, sand or sandy soil, not completely dry. Plants from the dry areas of North and Central America (see page 58). Sunning spots and UV lighting. Sun terrarium. *Temperature:* By day exactly 95°F (35°C), and the animals must be able to creep into cooler places; by night 59°F (15°C). Pseudo-winter rest from November to February at 59° to 69°F (15–20°C; reflector lamps not turned on). *Humidity:* 50 to 70 percent. *Food:* Insects, spiders, baby mice, also occasionally leaves and flowers. Drinking water will be licked from the decorations or from shallow saucers; spray plants with water once daily.

Tropidurine lizard
Photograph page 53
Tropidurus torquatus (Wied, 1820)
Total length: 10 inches (25 cm). *Head-torso length:* 4 inches (10 cm).
Distribution and Description: Northern South America. *Habitat:* Mountains to 3,100 feet (1,000 m); the edges of sparse forests in largely dry areas. *Identifying characteristics:* Spiny tail scales. *Behavior:* Diurnal. Inhabits ground and tree trunks. Dominant males on display spots.
Maintenance: Terrarium 60 × 24 × 24 inches (150 × 60 × 60 cm) for two males and four females. *Decoration:* Stones, stumps, sand or sandy soil, not completely dry. Plants from the dry areas of South America (see page 00). Sunning spots and UV lighting. Sun terrarium. *Temperature:* By day exactly 95°F (35°C), and the animals must be able to crawl into cooler places; by night 59°F (15°C). *Humidity:* 50 to 70 percent. *Food:* Insects, spiders, baby mice, occasionally also vegetarian fare. Drinking water will be licked from the decorations or from shallow saucers; spray plants with water once daily.

Common iguana *
Photographs page 35, inside back cover, back cover.
Iguana iguana (Linnaeus, 1758)
Endangered species designation: WA II
Total length: 80 inches (200 cm). *Head-torso length:* 20 inches (50 cm).
Distribution and Description: Southern Mexico to central South America. *Habitat:* Tropical rain forests and savannahs, always in close vicinity to water, with only small populations in the precipitation-poor coastal areas. *Identifying characteristics:* Large dewlap with a crest. Crest from neck to tail. Long, sharp claws. *Behavior:* Diurnal. Tree-dwelling. Likes to swim. Movements mostly quiet and balanced, therefore requires less space than its size might suggest. Usually lives in large groups. Can become tame; recognized people are greeted with nodding head.

Setting up Desert, Rain-Forest, and Water Terrariums

Maintenance: Changing terrarium size because as animals grow, more room is needed. For three juveniles: $40 \times 24 \times 24$ inches ($100 \times 60 \times 60$ cm); for one male and two females about 60 inches (150 cm) long: $80 \times 60 \times 60$ inches ($200 \times 150 \times 150$ cm). *Decorations:* Branches for climbing, at least as thick in diameter as the lizard's torso. Water holders for bathing. Floor surface that can be dampened for constant humidity. No plants. Sunning spots and UV lighting. Sun terrarium. *Temperature:* 77° to 95°F (25–35°C) during the day; 68° to 72°F (20–22°C) during the night. *Humidity:* 60 to 90 percent. *Food:* Juvenile animals eat animal fare for the most part: insects, earthworms, baby mice; some iguanas also eat fish. Vegetable fare (weeds, grasses, fruit, carrots, rice) is eaten during the growth period of the larger lizards and particularly by sexually mature animals. Many iguanas even give up animal food completely. Provide adequate amounts of vitamin and mineral supplements during the growth period because rickets, convulsive trembling, and other metabolic problems often cause irreparable damage to this species.

Common basilisk

Basiliscus basiliscus (Linnaeus, 1758)
Total length: 32 inches (80 cm). *Head-torso length:* 10 inches (25 cm).
Distribution and Description: Southern Central America. *Habitat:* Tropical rain forest, always in the vicinity of water. *Identifying characteristics:* Male has a casque, back and tail crests. Long extremities. Toes have fringes of skin. *Behavior:* Diurnal. Tree-dwelling. Likes to swim. Shy, reacts excitably, fast and powerful jumper, can also

move on two legs (see page 5). Lives in loose groups.
Maintenance: High terrarium, $36 \times 36 \times 50$ inches ($90 \times 90 \times 12$ cm) for one male and three females. For every additional animal of another species, add 2 inches (5 cm) more to each measurement. *Decorations:* Branches for climbing, stumps, water containers for swimming. Hard-leaved plants (the sharp claws destroy tender leaves) from the rain forest of Central and South America (see page 58). Sunning spots and UV lighting. *Temperature:* By day 77° to 86°F (25–30°C); by night 68° to 77°F (20–25°C) *Humidity:* 60 to 90 percent. *Food:* Insects and spiders, freshwater fish, earthworms, baby mice; in the natural habitat also small reptiles, frogs, and baby birds. Some common basilisks also eat vegetable food.

Double-crested basilisk

Photographs front cover
Basiliscus plumifrons (Cope, 1876) cover (inside), page 8
Total length: 28 inches (70 cm) *Head-torso length:* 8 inches (20 cm).
Distribution and Description: Central and southern Central America. *Habitat:* Tropical rain forests, always in the vicinity of water. *Identifying characteristics:* Males have crest on forehead, casque, and a back and tail crest; females have only suggestions. Long extremities. Toes have a fringe of skin. *Behavior:* Diurnal. Tree-dwelling. Likes to swim. Shy, excitable, fast and powerful jumper, can also move on two legs (see page 5). Lives in loose groups. Females also respond aggressively.
Maintenance: High terrarium, $36 \times 36 \times 50$ inches ($90 \times 90 \times 120$ cm) for one male and

Setting up Desert, Rain-Forest, and Water Terrariums

three females. For each additional animal, add 2 inches (5 cm) more to each measurement. *Decorations:* Branches for climbing, stumps, water containers for swimming. Hard-leaved plants (the sharp claws destroy tender leaves) from the rain forests of Central and South America (see page 58). Sunning places and UV lighting. *Temperature:* By day 77° to 86°F (25–30°C). *Humidity:* 60 to 90 percent. *Food:* Insects and spiders, freshwater fish, earthworms, baby mice; in natural habitat also small reptiles, frogs, and baby birds. Some double-crested basilisks also eat vegetable food.

Banded basilisk
Basiliscus vittatus (Wiegmann, 1828)
Total length: 30 inches (75 cm). *Head-torso length:* 8 inches (20 cm).
Distribution and Description: Central America. *Habitat:* Tropical rain forests, always in close vicinity to water. *Identifying characteristics:* Males have casque. Shallow back crest. Long extremities. Toes with skin fringe. *Behavior:* Diurnal. Tree-dwelling. Likes to swim. Shy, reacts excitedly, fast and powerful jumper, also can move on two legs (see page 5). Lives in loose groups.
Maintenance: High terrarium, 36 × 36 × 50 inches (90 × 90 × 120 cm) for one male and three females; for each additional animal add 2 inches (5 cm) to each measurement. *Decorations:* Branches for climbing, stumps, water containers for swimming. Hard-leaved plants (the sharp claws injure tender leaves) from the rain forests of Central and South America (see page 58). Sunning spots and UV lighting. *Temperature:* by day 77° to 86°F (25–30°C); by night 68° to 77°F (20–25°C). *Humidity:* 60 to 90 percent. *Food:*

Insects and spiders, freshwater fish, earthworms, baby mice; in natural habitat also small reptiles, frogs, and baby birds. Some banded basilisks also eat vegetable food.

Carolina anole
Photograph page 53
Anolis carolinensis (Duméril and Bibron, 1837)
Total length: 8 inches (22 cm). *Head-torso length:* 3 inches (7 cm).
Distribution and Description: Southeastern North America. *Habitat:* Woods, brush country, and cultivated land; also areas of human settlement. *Identifying characteristics:* Adhesive lamellae. *Behavior:* Diurnal. Inhabits trees and bushes. Lives in colonies.
Maintenance: High terrarium, 16 × 16 × 24 inches (40 × 40 × 60 cm) for one male and two females. For every two additional animals add 2 inches (5 cm) more to each measurement. *Decorations:* Branches and plenty of plants from the rain forests of North, Central, and South America (see page 58). Sunning spots and UV lighting. *Temperature:* By day 77° to 86°F (25–30°C); by night 65° to 74°F (18–23°C). Pseudo-winter rest from November to February at 59° to 68°F (15–20°C; reflector lamp not turned on). *Humidity:* 50 to 80 percent. *Food:* Insects and spiders, ripe fruit from time to time. Drinking water will be licked from plants; spray plants with water once daily.

Knight anole
Photograph page 53
Anolis equestris (Merrem, 1820)
Total length: 22 inches (55 cm). *Head-torso length:* 9 inches (20 cm).
Distribution and Description: Cuba, but it has spread, for instance, to Florida. *Habitat:* Rain forests. *Identifying characteristics:*

Setting up Desert, Rain-Forest, and Water Terrariums

Adhesive lamellae. *Behavior:* Diurnal. Tree-dwelling. More relaxed and less active than other species of anoles. Lives in loose groups.

Maintenance: High terrarium, $24 \times 24 \times 36$ inches ($60 \times 60 \times 90$ cm) for one male and two females. *Decorations:* Branches and stumps, plants from the rain forests of Central and South America (see page 58). Sunning spots and UV lighting. *Temperature:* By day 77° to 86°F (25–30°C); by night 68° to 77°F (20–25°C). *Humidity:* 60 to 90 percent. *Food:* Insects and spiders, baby mice; in natural habitat lizards, too. Because these lizards are slow eaters, it is best to feed each one individually, preferably with the help of tweezers; otherwise too many of the food insects escape into the decorations and the food intake cannot be controlled. Drinking water will be licked off the leaves or from the wells provided by the bromeliads; spray plants with water once a day.

Bahama anole

Anolis sagrei (Duméril and Bibron, 1837)
Total length: 8 inches (20 cm). *Head-torso length:* 3 inches (7 cm).
Distribution and Description: Orginally only the Bahamas, now also Central America, the Greater Antilles, and Florida. *Habitat:* Forest edges, bushy areas, cultivated landscapes, also the vicinity of human settlements. *Identifying characteristics:* Adhesive lamellae. *Behavior:* Diurnal. Lives in trees, bushes, ground, and stones. Lives in colonies.

Maintenance: High terrarium, $16 \times 16 \times 24$ inches ($40 \times 40 \times 60$ cm) for one male and two females; for every two additional animals add 2 inches (5 cm) to each measurement. *Decorations:* Branches and numerous plants from the rain forests of North, Central, and South America (see page 58). Sunning spots and UV lighting. *Temperature:* By day 77° to 86°F (25–30°C); by night 64° to 73°F (18–23°C). *Humidity:* 50 to 80 percent. *Food:* Insects and spiders, sometimes ripe fruit. Drinking water will be licked from the plants; spray them with water once daily.

Family: Agama (Agamidae)

Many typical features of the iguanas are present in the agamas in similar forms. Such parallel developments are called convergence. Dewlaps and crests are present in males usually. If they are present in both sexes, they are noticeably larger in the male. Also the body language, with head nodding or presentation of the flattened body, is like that of the iguanas. Typical of the agama is its "waving" during courtship (see page 42).

Differences between the sexes: The male has noticeably larger femoral and/or preanal pores (see page 41) than the female. To some extent the males are also differentiated from the females by their dewlaps and crests. In some species the sheaths for the hemipenis can be seen on the underside of the root of the tail; in others, particularly with young animals, differentiation between sexes is only possible with the use of a probe (see page 42).

Reproduction: All species are ovoviviparous (see page 45). The 4 to 20 eggs in a clutch are deposited in a hole in the ground. They must be transferred to an incubator. The gestation period is 60 to 100 days at a temperature of 81°F (29°C). Nurturing will be successful only if the young are cared for separately.

Setting up Desert, Rain-Forest, and Water Terrariums

General maintenance advice: Soa-soas and water dragons are nervous animals, quick to flee. They do not recognize glass and jump against it or constantly rub their snouts against it so that irreparable damage can be done to their lips and jaws. Make the glass visible with a stripe across it! With soa-soas and water dragons it is not possible to mix several males of the same species. The low-ranking animals will not be able to endure psychological stress and will die. But you can keep soa-soas and water dragons together in family groups.

Bearded lizard *
Amphibolurus barbatus (Cuvier, 1829)
Total length: 22 inches (5 cm). *Head-torso length:* 10 inches (25 cm).
Distribution and Description: Australia. *Habitat:* Brushy grasslands; thin, grassy woods. *Identifying characteristics:* Scales on head and neck are barbed, partly elongated into spines; they become raised during threat posture. *Behavior:* Diurnal. Lives on the ground, on stones and stumps. Lives in small groups, dominant males on display spots.
Maintenance: Terrarium, 60 × 24 × 28 inches (150 × 60 × 70 cm) for one male and two females. It is better to double the area and keep two males and four females because then the behavior patterns become more distinct. *Decorations:* Well arranged stones and stumps. Sand with damp areas for egg-laying. Plants from the dry areas of Australia (see page 61) are only possible in large terrariums. Sunning spots and UV lighting. *Temperature:* By day precisely 77° to 95°F (25–35°C), and the animals must be able to crawl into cooler areas; by night 65° to 68°F (18–20°C). Pseudo-winter rest from November to February at 59° to 68°F (15–20°C; reflector lamps not turned on). *Humidity:* 50 to 70 percent. *Food:* Insects and spiders, baby mice and baby rats; in natural habitat also small reptiles and amphibians. Vegetable food (leaves, flowers, and fruit) is sometimes also enjoyed. Drinking water is licked from the decorations or shallow saucers; spray plants with water once daily.

Oriental (Chinese) water dragon
Photograph on pages 10, 35
Physignathus concincinus (Cuvier, 1829)
Total length: 32 inches (80 cm). *Head-torso length:* 10 inches (25 cm).
Distribution and Description: *Habitat:* Tropical rain forests, always in close vicinity to water. It is not certain how high these agamas live; it is possible that populations from higher locations may be kept too warm in the terrarium. *Identifying characteristics:* Comb from neck to tail; in males this is noticeably large than in females. *Behavior:* Diurnal. Tree-dwelling. Flight behavior: Jumps into water and disappears. Lives in loose groups.
Maintenance: Terrarium 60 × 40 × 40 inches (150 × 100 × 100 cm) for one male and two females. *Decorations:* Branches for climbing. Large water containers; better yet, a water terrarium. Mature animals need to have a 6-inch (15-cm) depth of floor medium for egg-laying. Strong, tough-leaved plants from the rain forests of Southeast Asia (see page 59) are only recommended for very roomy terrariums because the lizards are heavy and also many of them eat leaves. Sunning places and UV lighting. *Temperature:* By day 77° to 86°F (25–30°C); by night 68° to 77°F (20–25°C). *Humidity:* 80 to 90 percent. *Food:* Insects, earthworms, freshwater fish, baby

75

Setting up Desert, Rain-Forest, and Water Terrariums

rats, and mice; in the wild also small reptiles, amphibians, and bird nestlings. Some also like weeds, fruit, carrots, and rice.

Soa-soa

Hydrosaurus amboinensis (Schlosser, 1768) Photograph, front cover
Total length: 44 inches (110 cm). *Head-torso length:* 14 inches (35 cm)
Distribution and Description: Sulawesi (Celebes). It is not clear whether the soa-soa of the Moluccas, Philippines, and western New Guinea belong to the species of *Hydrosaurus amboinensis* or if it is a separate species. *Habitat:* Tropical rain forests, always in close vicinity to water. *Identifying characteristics:* Crest from neck to tail, where there is an especially large "sail"; in females the crest is small and there is no "sail." Toes have a fringe of skin. *Behavior:* Diurnal. Tree-dwelling. Flight pattern is not to tops of trees but plunging into water and disappearing or fleeing on two legs (see page 5). Reacts excitedly. Powerful jumper. Lives in loose groups.
Maintenance: Terrarium $60 \times 40 \times 40$ inches $(150 \times 100 \times 100$ cm) for one male and two females. *Decorations:* Branches for climbing. Large water containers or, better yet, a water terrarium. Mature animals need to have a 6-inch (15-cm) floor medium for egg-laying. Sunning places and UV lighting. *Temperature:* By day 77° to 86°F (25 – 30°C); by night 68° to 77°F (20 – 25°C). *Humidity:* 80 to 90 percent. *Food:* Insects, earthworms, freshwater fish, baby rats and mice; in natural habitat also small reptiles, amphibians, and bird nestlings. Vegetable food consists of weeds, fruit, carrots, and rice.

Angle-headed Agama

Acanthosaura crucigera (Boulenger, 1885) Photograph, page 35
Total length: 11 inches (27 cm). *Head-torso length:* 4 inches (10 cm).
Distribution and Description: Indochina, Malay peninsula. *Habitat:* Fog-dampened mountain forests and tea plantations up to elevations of 2,600 feet (800 m). *Identifying characteristics:* Sharp-spined neck and back comb. *Behavior:* Diurnal. Lives in trees and bushes. Lives in loose groups.
Maintenance: Cube-shaped terrarium, $24 \times 24 \times 24$ inches $(60 \times 60 \times 60$ cm) for four lizards. *Decorations:* Branches, twigs, bark, plenty of plants from the rain forest of Southeast Asia (see page 59). Sunning spots and UV lighting. *Temperature:* By day 68° to 77°F (20 – 25°C); by night 59° to 68°F (15 – 20°C). *Humidity:* In the morning 100 percent (spray cool water early and then later turn on warming lamps), otherwise 70 to 90 percent. *Food:* Insects and spiders. Drinking water will be licked from the plants; spray plants with water once daily.

Bornean bloodsucker

Calotes cristatellus (Kuhl, 1820)
Total length: 20 inches (50 cm). *Head-torso length:* 4 inches (10 cm).
Distribution and Description: Indochina, Indo-Malayan archipelago to western New Guinea. *Habitat:* Low-lying areas of light forest, cultivated land, human dwellings. *Identifying characteristics:* Spiny neck and back combs. Throat skin can be puffed up. *Behavior:* Diurnal. Lives on tree trunks, branches, and leaves. Usually placid but reacts to disturbance with great fear and flees in a panic. Lives in loose groups.

Setting up Desert, Rain-Forest, and Water Terrariums

Maintenance: Terrarium, 40 × 24 × 24 inches (100 × 60 × 60 cm) for four lizards. *Decorations:* Branches, twigs, bark, plenty of plants from the rain forests of southeast Asia (see page 59). Caution: Do not use any forked pieces of wood: they are a danger to tails! Sunning spots and UV lighting. *Temperature:* By day 77° to 86°F (25 – 30°C); by night 68° to 77°F (20 – 25°C). *Humidity:* 60 to 90 percent. *Food:* Insects, spiders, baby mice. Drinking water will be licked from the plants; spray them with water once daily.

Family: Skink (Scincidae)

Skinks have a cylindrical body with mostly smooth, shining scales. Because the limbs are very short, even missing in some species, skinks progress with a creeping motion so that they are often confused with snakes.

Differences between the sexes: Femoral and preanal pores are missing; other secondary sex characteristics are only seldom present. An imprecise way of determining sex is the comparison of skull and tail size. The skull of the male is somewhat larger and fuller than that of the female; the underside of the male tail is somewhat thickened at the base. Sex differentiation through the analysis of testosterone may be a useful method, but it has not been tested well enough yet.

Reproduction: Most species are ovoviviparous (see page 45). Some have a juvenile skin in the period just after hatching to protect them from being eaten by their parents.

General maintenance advice: Skinks, which are generally peaceful and rather inactive when kept in isolation, would need little living space if the species were not so aggressive with each other. If you need to make a separation to keep the peace, remove the dominant, stronger animal because the submissive one will be at an advantage if there is a recombination later.

Gerrard's blue-tongued skink *
Tilqua gerrardii (Gray, 1845)
Photograph page 64.

Total length: 14 inches (35 cm). *Head-torso length:* 7 inches (18 cm).

Distribution and Description: Eastern Australia (from south of the Cape York peninsula, southward to the middle of the New South Wales). *Habitat:* Rain forests. *Identifying characteristics:* On both sides of the lower jaw there is a greatly enlarged back tooth for breaking snail shells. *Behavior:* Diurnal but also often remains hidden all day long. Inhabits ground, stumps, low-growing copses. For the most part lives on its own but is usually sociable in a group. Ovoviviparous.

Maintenance: Terrarium 40 × 20 × 20 inches (100 × 50 × 50 cm) for four lizards. *Decorations:* Branches, stumps, plants from the rain forests of Australia (see page 61). UV lighting off and on. *Temperature:* By day 77° to 82°F (25 – 28°C); by night 68° to 77°F (20 – 25°C). *Humidity:* 60 to 90 percent. *Food:* Snails and as a suitable substitute food, prepared cat food. Because of the high concentrations of vitamins A and D in commercial cat and dog foods, they must be fed sparingly, rather than as staples of the captive lizards' diet. Drinking water will be licked from the plants; spray plants with water once daily.

Blue-tongued skink
Photograph page 64
Tilqua gigas (Schneider, 1801)

Setting up Desert, Rain-Forest, and Water Terrariums

Total length: 22 inches (55 cm). *Head-torso length:* 12 inches (30 cm).
Distribution and Description: New Guinea. *Habitat:* Grassy forests. *Identifying characteristics:* Blue tongue. *Behavior:* Diurnal. Lives in ground, stumps, and stones. Likes to dig in ground. Solitary usually, very aggressive when first placed with others. Ovoviviparous.
Maintenance: Terrarium 60 × 28 × 20 inches (150 × 70 × 50 cm) for three lizards. *Decorations:* Stones, stumps, well arranged rubble. Caves and hollows with emergency exits. No living plants, only dry branches or grasses, since blue-tongued skinks like to dig. Sunning places and UV lighting. Sun terrarium. *Temperature:* By day 77° to 90°F (25 – 32°C); by night 64° to 72°F (18 – 22°C). Pseudo-winter rest from November to February at 64° to 72°F (18 – 22°C reflector lamps not turned on). *Humidity:* 50 to 75 percent. *Food:* Snails, insects, freshwater fish, baby rats and mice; in natural habitat, small reptiles and amphibians as well. Some animals also like weeds, fruit, carrots, rice. Drinking water is licked from the decorations or from shallow saucers.

Spiny-tailed skink *
Egernia cunninghami (Gray, 1845)
Photographs pages 9 and 64
Total length: 14 inches (25 cm). *Head-torso length:* 6 inches (16 cm).
Distribution and Description: Southeastern Australia. *Habitat:* Dry bush country, rocky slopes. *Identifying characteristics:* Scales are ridged or "keeled." *Behavior:* Diurnal. Lives in ground, stones, stumps. Likes to burrow in ground. Lives in loose groups. Ovoviviparous.
Maintenance: Shallow terrarium,

48 × 24 × 20 inches (120 × 60 × 50 cm) for three lizards. *Decorations:* Stones, stumps, well constructed rock piles. Caves and hollows with emergency exits. No living plants but only dried branches or grasses, because the animals like to dig. Sunning places and UV lighting. Sun terrarium. *Temperature:* By day 77° to 90°F (25 – 32°C); by night 64° to 72°F (18 – 22°C). From November to February, pseudo-winter rest at 59° to 68°F (15 – 20°C; reflector lamps not turned on). *Humidity:* 50 to 75 percent. *Food:* Snails, insects, freshwater fish, baby rats and mice; in natural habitat, small reptiles and amphibians also. Some animals also like weeds, fruit, carrots, rice. Drinking water is licked from the decorations or from shallow saucers.

Five-lined skink
Eumeces fasciatus (Linnaeus, 1758)
Photograph page 64
Total length: 9 inches (22 cm). *Head-torso length:* 4 inches (10 cm).
Distribution and Description: Eastern North America. *Habitat:* Woods, brush country. *Identifying characteristics:* During courtship the head of the male turns red. *Behavior:* Inhabits ground, stumps, underbrush, sometimes also tree-dwelling. Mostly lives on its own. Ovoviviparous. Female guards the eggs.
Maintenance: Terrarium 20 × 20 × 20 inches (50 × 50 × 50 cm) for five lizards. *Decorations:* Stumps, branches, brush. Plants from the temperate zones of the Americas (see page 58). *Temperature:* Because of the very broad north-south expanse of the distribution area, the climate zones are very different. (Ask where the animal comes from at the time of purchase.) By day 64° to 86°F (18 –

Setting up Desert, Rain-Forest, and Water Terrariums

30°C); by night 54° to 64°F (12 – 18°C) Pseudo-winter rest from November to February at 59° to 68°F (15 – 20°C; reflector lamps not turned on). *Humidity:* 60 to 90 percent. *Food:* Insects and spiders, occasionally snails. Drinking water is licked from the plants; spray them with water once daily.

Mabuya quinquetaeniata
(Lichtenstein, 1823)
Photograph page 64
Total length: 10 inches (25 cm). *Head-torso length:* 4 inches (9 cm).
Distribution and Description: Africa, south from the Sahara to the Kalahari desert. *Habitat:* Savannahs, briar-covered plains, and thin woods. *Identifying characteristics:* Skin color pales at sexual maturity; males are then almost entirely brown. *Behavior:* Diurnal. Inhabits ground, stones, stumps, occasionally also trees. Swims now and then. Lives in loose groups.
Maintenance: Terrarium 20 × 20 × 20 inches (50 × 50 × 50 cm) for four lizards. *Decorations:* Stones, stumps, branches, twigs. Water container. Plants from Africa (see page 60). Sunning places and UV lighting. *Temperature:* By day 77° to 95°F (25 – 35°C); by night 64° to 68°F (18 – 20°C). *Humidity:* 50 to 80 percent. *Food:* Insects, spiders, baby mice; occasionally ripe fruit.

Family: Whiptails (Teiidae)

The stomach scales of the Teiidae are much larger than those of other lizards.
Differences between sexes: In the sexually mature male the head is somewhat broader and foreshortened and the femoral pores (see page 41) are much more noticeably prominent than in the female. The base of the tail of the male is thickened by the presence of the hemipenis sheath. A definite determination of sex, particularly for juveniles, is only possible with the use of a probe (see page 42).

Reproduction: In nature tegus lay their eggs in termite hills, which not only protects them from predators but also provides them with a constantly maintained temperature. Jungle runners bury their eggs in the ground. Eggs laid in the terrarium must be transferred to an incubator. Some species of these lizards are parthenogenetic; in a few of these, only females are known to exist; in others, males are rare. In the wholly parthenogenetic species, the females do not require fertilization by males to produce viable eggs. When they hatch, all the baby lizards from these lizards are, of course, female.

General maintenance advice: In their search for hiding places whiptails dig vigorously and fling the earth quite far in the process. Therefore the earth floor of the terrarium should consist of leafmold or evergreen-needle mold and, to avoid the danger of broken glass, should contain no stones.

Whiptails are solitary; a collection of several therefore depends on the behavior of the individuals. To separate an aggressive animal from a submissive one or to separate a female that wants to lay eggs, you can divide the terrarium as necessary with a fence. In that case, however, it is important to maintain constant sight contact and the possibility for the animals to touch each other with their tongues. This will simplify recombining them later.

Setting up Desert, Rain-Forest, and Water Terrariums

Jungle runner
Ameiva ameiva (Linnaeus, 1758)
Total length: 20 inches (50 cm). *Head-torso length:* 6 inches (15 cm).
Distribution and Description: Central America southward to the mouth of the Rio de la Plata in South America; naturalized in Florida. *Habitat:* Grassy forests, bush country, high grass. *Identifying characteristics:* Pointed head, cleft tongue. *Behavior:* Diurnal. Inhabits ground, stumps, and low branches. Likes to dig. Solitary.
Maintenance: Terrarium 48 × 24 × 24 inches(120 × 60 × 60 cm) for five lizards. *Decoration:* Branches, stumps, twigs, plentiful plants from Central and South America (see page 00); protect plant roots by planting in a wire basket. Sunning places and UV lighting. *Temperature:* By day 77° to 86°F (25 – 30°C); by night 68° to 77°F (20 – 25°C). *Humidity:* 60 to 80 percent. *Food:* Insects and spiders, baby mice, earthworms, eggs; some animals also like fruit. Drinking water will be licked from the plants.

Tegu *
Tupinambis teguixin nigropunctatus (Spix, 1825)
Photograph page 54
Endangered species designation: WA II
Total length: 48 inches (120 cm). *Head-torso length:* 20 inches (50 cm).
Distribution: North and central South America. *Habitat:* Thin forests with thick underbrush. *Identifying characteristics:* Cleft tongue. *Behavior:* Diurnal. Lives in ground and stumps. Likes to dig. Solitary.
Maintenance: Shallow terrarium, 80 × 40 × 28 inches (200 × 100 × 70 cm), for one male and two females. *Decorations:*

Branches, stumps, large stones. Water containers for swimming. Only rugged plants from Central and South America (see page 58), their root balls protected by a wire basket. Sunning places and UV lighting. *Temperature:* By day 77° to 82° F (25 – 28°C); by night 68° to 77°F (20 – 25°C). *Humidity:* 60 to 90 percent. *Food:* Insects, earthworms, baby and later grown mice, freshwater fish, eggs, fruit; in natural habitat also small reptiles and amphibians.

Family: True lizards (Lacertidae)

Some genera of this family, to which the lizards described belong, are also called collared lizards. They are differentiated from other lizards by a horizontal fold between the throat and the chest scales. At the back end of this fold the scales are noticeably enlarged. True lizards are among those that are able to discard their tails to deceive a pursuer. A typical submissive gesture is treading.
Differences between the sexes: The males always have distinctly prominent femoral pores (see page 41) and a thicker tail base than the female.
Reproduction: While the male of the Canary Islands lizards bites the neck of the female during copulation, the male of the Pityuses lizards bites the flank. Up to three egg clutches are buried every year in a damp place in the ground. The eggs must be transferred to the incubator because only there can constant humidity be guaranteed.

Canary Islands lizard *
Gallotia galloti (Duméril and Bibron, 1839)
Photograph page 63

Setting up Desert, Rain-Forest, and Water Terrariums

Total length: 18 inches (45 cm). *Head-torso length:* 5 inches (12 cm).
Distribution and Description: Canary Islands; there are subspecies on individual islands. *Habitat:* Fields of scree, borders of cultivated land. *Identifying characteristics:* Cleft tongue. Sexually mature males have blue spots on neck and flanks. Juvenile females have stripes. *Behavior:* Diurnal. Lives in ground and rock falls. Males are sometimes very territorial.
Maintenance: Terrarium, 48 × 20 × 20 inches (120 × 50 × 50 cm), for one male and three females. *Decorations:* Stones and lava, though not firmly fixed because they must be removable for cleaning. Sand with damp areas for egg-laying. Plants from the Canary Islands (see page 00). Sunning places and UV lighting. Sun terrarium. *Temperature:* By day exactly 77° to 95°F (25 – 35°C); by night 64°F (18°C). Pseudo-winter rest from November to February at 59° to 68°F (15 – 20°C; reflector lamps not turned on). *Humidity:* 50 to 70 percent. *Food:* Insects are only occasionally eaten by young animals; otherwise worms, snails, baby mice, fruit, seeds, weeds (also dried), honey, rice, occasionally pudding and yogurt. Water will be licked from the decorations or from shallow saucers.

Pityuses lizard *
Podarcis pityusensis (Bosca, 1883)
Photograph page 63
Endangered species regulation: WA II
Total length: 8 inches (20 cm). *Head-torso length:* 3 inches (7 cm).
Distribution and Description: Pityuses Islands: Ibiza, Formentera, and others, with subspecies on the particular islands. *Habitat:* Fields of rockfall and sandy regions with sparse growth, stone fences, human dwellings. *Identifying characteristics:* Typical lizard. Forked tongue. *Behavior:* Diurnal. Lives in ground and among stones. Lives in colonies.
Maintenance: Terrarium 40 × 20 × 20 inches (100 × 50 × 50 cm), for six lizards. *Decoration:* Sand, stones, rubble, and dry grass, well arranged. Plants of the Mediterranean area (see page 61). Sunning spots and UV lighting. Sun terrarium. *Temperature:* By day precisely 77° to 95° F (25 – 35°C); by night 64°F (18°C). During the months from December to February a winter rest at 46° to 57°F (8 – 14°C); reflector lamps not turned on. *Humidity:* 50 to 70 percent. *Food:* Insects and spiders, fruit, weeds, honey, rice, yogurt and pudding. Drinking water will be licked from the decorations; spray plants with water once daily.

Family: Lateral Fold Lizards (Anguidae)

To this family belongs the southern alligator lizard described below, which is related to the European anguine lizards and has a similarly shy life style. However, the southern alligator lizard has well-developed limbs.
Differences between the sexes: The males can often be recognized by the thickened tail base because of the hemipenis sheath. Only an examination by probe will determine for sure, however.
Reproduction: Species that live in mountains are ovoviviparous because of the extreme climate; those at lower elevations are oviparous. After egg-laying the female lies on top of the clutch and guards it. Eggs laid

Setting up Desert, Rain-Forest, and Water Terrariums

in the terrarium must, however, be transferred to the incubator to guarantee certain maturation.

Southern alligator lizard *

Gerrhonotus multicarinatus (Blainville, 1835) Photograph on page 63
Total length: 16 inches (40 cm). *Head-torso length:* 6 inches (16 cm).
Distribution and Description: Western North America, from southern Washington to Baja California, in various subspecies. *Habitat:* Lives in light woods, prairies, and canyons with moderately damp floors.
Identifying characteristics: Deep side folds; they do not signal inadequate nourishment.
Behavior: Diurnal. Inhabits ground, stones, trees. Oviparous. Nurtures young. Lives in loose groups.
Maintenance: Terrarium, 40 × 20 × 24 inches (100 × 50 × 60 cm), for one male and three females. *Decorations:* Stones, stumps, well arranged branches for climbing. Sandy leafmold or pine-needle mold. Plants from the dry areas of North America (see page 58). Sunning spots and UV lighting. *Temperature:* By day 77° to 89°F (25 – 30°C); by night 59° to 64°F (15 – 18°C). For subspecies from the northern part of the distribution area, a winter rest. If the origins are not known, pseudo-rest period from November to February at 59° to 68°F (15 – 20°C; reflector lamps not turned on). *Humidity:* 60 to 80 percent. *Food:* Shell-less snails, slugs, insects, spiders, baby mice; in natural habitat also eggs and baby birds. Drinking water is licked from the decorations.

Family: Monitors (Varanidae)

Many characteristics of monitors remind one of snakes. The motion is slithering, although these lizards possess four muscular extremities. The deeply cleft tongue is continually stretched out to take up scent particles. When the throat is expanded, large pieces of food can be swallowed whole. Moreover, they display some mutual anatomic features that suggest their kinship with snakes, particularly to the giant snakes.

The monitor family contains the largest lizards, ranging from the Komodo dragons, which can be as long as 10 feet (3 m), to the "dwarfs" of scarcely 12 inches (3 cm). Just considering the smaller ones, species native to Australia are not in trade because strict laws forbid their export. As a consequence, all monitors are listed in WA II C2.
Differences between sexes: It is seldom possible to tell the sex of monitors from external characteristics, such as the insignificantly fatter skull and the thicker tail base of the male. The only sure way is examination with a probe (see page 42). Often both tips of the hemipenis will protrude during the passing of feces.
Reproduction: The eggs — there may be as many as 50 — are buried in the earth; in its natural habitat, the Nile monitor lays them in a termite mound. In the terrarium the clutch of newly laid eggs must be transferred to the incubator so that they do not fall prey to the predatory parents. All the larger monitors are predators and are particularly eager for the eggs of crocodiles and turtles. The maturation period lasts for about 110 to 200 days at 84°F (29°C).

Setting up Desert, Rain-Forest, and Water Terrariums

Advice for general maintenance: Most monitors are solitary; keeping several in a terrarium therefore depends on individual behavior. A sliding partition for separating the animals should therefore be part of the terrarium plan and arranged in advance. Not to isolate the animals completely, a side of screen is recommended because visual contact and a chance for tongue touching will facilitate recombining the lizards later.

Water-dependent species need roomy swimming containers, which should measure in length at least twice the head-torso measurement of the largest lizard, in width one-half the head-torso measurement. When you are keeping large animals, you are well advised not to use a floor medium because the splashing of the water from the swimming pool and the usually energetic flight through the water will soak the terrarium floor. And then, too, the water will stay free of floor medium. If egg-laying is anticipated, then a container with suitable material must be introduced.

Warning: Be particularly careful in dealing with monitors: they can give you very deep bites. Newly introduced animals are especially frightened and move terrifically fast. They can escape while you are working in the terrarium and then must be captured again. A monitor that feels itself threatened not only uses its teeth as weapons but also its tail and claws. The climbing species have particular sharp claws and can inflict their keepers with wounds that take a long time to heal.

Nile monitor *

Varanus niloticus (Linnaeus, 1758)
Photograph page 54
Endangered species regulation: WA II C2
Total length: 80 inches (200 cm). *Head-torso length:* 32 inches (80 cm).
Distribution and Description: Africa south of the Sahara. *Habitat:* Thin forests, savannahs, and steep banks, always in close vicinity to water. *Identifying characteristics:* Slender head. Nostrils somewhat in the middle between the end of the snout and the eye. *Behavior:* Diurnal. Inhabits water, ground, and trees. Solitary.
Maintenance: Water terrarium, 80 × 60 × 60 inches (200 × 150 × 150 cm), for one male and one female. *Decoration:* Branches for climbing. For young animals only, plants from Africa (see page 60). Sunning places and UV lighting. *Temperature:* By day 77° to 86°F (25 – 30°C); by night 64° to 68°F (18 – 20°C). *Humidity:* 70 to 90 percent. *Food:* In the juvenile phase, insects; later, freshwater fish, mice, rats, chicks, eggs; in natural habitat also reptiles, amphibians, and large snails.

Cape monitor *

Varanus exanthematicus (Bosca, 1792)
Photograph page 54
Endangered species regulation: WA II C
Total length: 60 inches (150 cm). *Head-torso length:* 28 inches (70 cm).
Distribution and Description: In many subspecies Africa, south of the Sahara, but not West Africa. *Habitat:* Dry savannahs, briary plains, rocky landscapes, also in higher elevations. *Identifying characteristics:* Head short and plump. Nostril directly in front of the eye. *Behavior:* Diurnal. Lives in the ground, in rock heaps, boulders. Likes to dig. Solitary.

Setting up Desert, Rain-Forest, and Water Terrariums

Maintenance: Shallow terrarium, 80 × 60 × 40 inches (200 × 150 × 100 cm), for one male and one female. *Decorations:* Sandy floor, no pebbles. which would be flung against glass. Well-fastened stone piles and clay pipes sunk into floor for caves, stumps. Small water container or keep the floor of the caves damp. Sunning places and UV lighting. Sun terrarium. *Temperature:* By day precisely 77° to 95°F (25 – 35°C); by night 59° to 68°F (15 – 20°C). For animals from the southern distribution area, pseudo-winter rest from November to February at 59° to 68°F (15 – 20°C; reflector lamps not turned on). *Humidity:* 50 to 80 percent. *Food:* In the juvenile phase, insects; later, mice, rats, chicks, eggs, and after becoming accustomed to them, freshwater fish.

Books for Further Help

General Referencs

Behler, J.L. *The Audubon Society Field Guide to North American Reptiles and Amphibians.* New York; Knopf, 1979.

Conant, R. *A Field Guide to Reptiles and Amphibians of Eastern North America.* Boston: Houghton Mifflin, 1958.

Cooper, J.E., and Jackson, O.F. *Diseases of the Reptilia.* London and New York: Academic Press, 1981.

Grzimek, B. (ed.). *Grzimek's Animal Life Encyclopedia, Vol. 6., Reptiles.* New York: Van Nostrand-Reinhold Co., 1972.

Hoff, G.L., Frye, F.L., and Jacobson, E.R. (eds.). *Diseases of Amphibians and Reptiles.* New York: Plenum, 1984.

Burton, M. (ed.). *The New Larousse Encyclopedia of Animal Life.* New York: Bonanza Books, 1981.

Marcus, L.C. *Veterinary Biology and Medicine of Captive Amphibians and Reptiles.* Philadelphia: Lea & Febiger, 1981.

Smith, H.M., and Brodie, E.D., Jr. *Reptiles of North America.* New York: Golden Press, 1982.

Stebbins, R.C. *A Field Guide to Western Reptiles and Amphibians of Western North America.* Boston: Houghton Mifflin, 1966.

Newsletters and Journals

Bulletin of the Chicago Herpetological Society
2001 N. Clark Street
Chicago, Illinois 60614

Bulletin of the Marylana Herpetological Society
Department of Herpetology
Natural History Society of Maryland
2643 North Charles Street
Baltimore, Maryland 21218

Kansas Herpetological Society Newsletter
Museum of Natural History
University of Kansas
Lawrence, Kansas 66045

Northern California Herpetological Society
P.O. BOX 1363
Davis, California 95616-1363

Guides on Endangered Species

Ashton, R.E. (compiler), Edwards, S.R., and Pisani, G.R. *Endangered and Threatened Amphibians and Reptiles in the United States.* Society for the Study of Amphibians and Reptiles. Lawrence, Kansas; 1976.

Collins, J.T., Huheey, J.E., Knight, J.L., and Smith, H.M. *Standard Common and Current Scientific Names for North American Amphibians and Reptiles.* Society for the Study of Amphibians and Reptiles Herpetological Circular Number 7. Lawrence, Kansas, 1978.

Czajka, A.F., and Nickerson, M.A. *State Regulations for Collecting Reptiles and Amphibians.* Milwaukee, WI. Milwaukee Public Museum Special Publications in Biology and Geology, Number 1. 1974.

Index

Numerals in *italics* indicate color photographs

Acanthosaura crucigera, 35,
  76
Agamas, 74–75
Agave, 59
Aglaonema, 59
Alligators, 62
Aloe, 60
Ameiva ameiva, 80
American cockroach, 32
Amoebic dysentery, 51
Amphibolurus barbatus, 75
Angle-headed agama, 76
Angle-headed lizard, *35*
Animal food, 27–28
Anolis carolinensis, 53, 73
Anolis equestris, 53, 73–74
Anolis sagrei, 74
Anubias, 60
Artificial stones, 21
Artificial turf, 25
Asiatic house gecko, *36,* 66
Asparagus fern, 60
Autotomy, 6

Bahama anole, 74
Banded basilisk, 73
Barderian gland, 6
Basic care:
  body care, 38
  holding lizards, 38–39
  rules for keepers, 34
  stress avoidance, 39
  terrarium care, 37
  vacation care, 40
Basiliscus basiliscus, 72
Basiliscus plumifrons, 9,
  72–73
Basiliscus vittatus, 73
Basilisks, 69
Bearded lizard, 75
Behavior, 8, 11
Blechnum, 61
Blue-tongued skink, 77–78
Body care, 38
Body temperature, 7–8
Bornean bloodsucker, 76–77
Bottom heating, 16
Bowstring hemp, 60
Breeders, 24
Breeding:
  courtship, 42
  egg-laying, 43
  incubation, 43–44
  live-bearing lizards, 45
  mating, 42–43

  parents, 41
  sex determination, 41–42
  young animal, 44–45
Bromeliads, 58–59
Butcher's broom, 61

Calcium, 48
Calotes cristatellus, 76–77
Canary Islands date palm, 61
Canary Islands lizard, *63,*
  80–81
Cape monitor, *54,* 83–84
Care, *See* Basic care
Carnivorous lizards, 29
Carolina anole, *53,* 73
Chinese water dragon.
  See Oriental water
  dragon
Chlorophytum, 60
CITES.|*See*|Washington agreement
Climate control, 34
Cloaca, 43, 50
Clutch, 43
Cockroach, 32
Color change (skin), 7
Columnar cactus, 59
Common basilisk, 72
Common iguana, *35,* 71–72
Convulsive trembling, 48
Courtship, 42
Crickets, 32

Decayed pine needles, 56
Desert plants, 60–61
Desert terrarium:
  display places, 21–22
  egg-laying places, 22
  planting zones, 22
  stone decorations, 20–21
  water container, 21
Dewlap, 30, 68
Dieffenbachia, 58
Dimmer switch, 17
Display places, 21
Double-crested Basilisk, 9, 72–73|
Dracena, 60
Dwarf caiman, 62, 65
Dyckia, 59

Ears, 6
Echeveria, 59
Egernia cunninghami, 9, 78
Egg-binding, 50–51
Egg-laying, 43
Egg-laying places, 22

Egg tooth, 44
Electrical accidents, avoid-
  ance of, 15
Endangered species, 24
English ivy, 61
Epiphytes, 20, 56
Eublepharis macularis, 36,
  68
Eumeces fasciatus, 78–79
External wounds, 47
Eyelid swelling, 47–48
Eyes, 6

False aralia, 61
Fecal examination, 46
Feeding, 26
  animal food, 27–28
  force-feeding, 30
  minerals, 28
  plant food, 27
  proper feeding, 28–30
  vitamins, 28
Ficus, 59–60, 61
First feeding, 26, 44–45
Five-lined skink, 78–79
Floor material, 20
Fluorescent lamps, 16
Food animals, 33–35
Food supplements, 29–30
Force-feeding, 30
Freshwater fish, 27

Gallotia galloti, 63, 80–81
Gasteria, 60
Gecko gecko, 36, 68
Geckos, 65–68
Gerrard's blue-tongued skink,
  77
Gerrhonotus multicarinatus,
  63, 82
Ginger, 60
Gold dust Madagascar day
  gecko, 67
Grasses, 29
Grasshoppers, 31–32

Halogen vapor lamps, 17
Haworthia, 61
Heating, 15–16
Hechtia, 59
Hemidactylus frenatus, 36, 66
Hemipenes, 42
Herbivorous lizards, 28–29
Hiding places, 22
House leek, 61
Humidity control, 18, 36

Hydrosaurus amboinesis, 76
Hygrometer, 18

Iguana iguana, 35, 71–72
Iguanas, 68–70
Illness. *See* Sickness
Incubating medium, 44
Incubation, 43–44
Infrared lamps, 15–16
Insects, 28
Intestinal prolapse, 50
Intestinal tract
  Inflammation, 49–50

Jacobson's organ, 6
Jade plants, 60
Jaw suppuration, 48–49
Jungle runner, 80

Kangaroo vine, 61
Knight anole, *53,* 73–74

Lachrymal gland, 6
Lamellae, 5
Large Madagascar gecko, *36,*
  67–68
Large stone constructions, 21
Lateral fold lizards, 81–82
Leaf vegetables, 29
Leafmold, 56
Leopard gecko, *36,* 68
Lighting, 16–17
Live-bearing lizards, 45
Living insects, 29
Lizards:
  behavior, 8, 11
  body temperature, 7–8
  limbs, 5
  origins, 5
  sensory organs, 6
  skin, 7
  tail, 5–6

Mabuya quinquetaeniata, 79
Maggots, 52
Marantas, 59
Mating, 42–43
Mercury vapor lamps, 17
Metabolic bone disease, 48
Mexican spiny lizard, 53
Mice, 29, 35
Minerals, 28
Mites, 46–47
Mixing species, 39–40
Molting, 7
  problems, 47

Index

Monitors, 82–84
Mouthrot, 48–49
Myrtle, 61

Natural stone, 20–21
Nematodes, 52
Nictitating membrane, 6
Nile monitor, *54*, 83

Oleander, 61
Opuntia, 59
Oriental (Chinese) water
  dragon, *10, 35,* 75–76
Oviparity, 45
Ovoviviparity, 45

Paleosuchus palpebrosus, 65
Panther gecko, *36*
Parents, 41
Penis prolapse, 50
Peperomia, 59
Pet stores, 24
Phelsuma laticauda, 67
Phelsuma lineata, 67
Phelsuma madagascariensis,
  36, 67–68
Philodendrons, 58
Phlebodium, 59
Physignathus concincinus,
  10, 35, 75–76
Pityuses lizard, 63, 81
Plant food, 27
Plant lice, 29
Planting medium, 56
Planting zones, 22
Plants (terrarium):
  from Africa, 60–61
  from the Americas, 58–59
  from Australia, 61
  changing, 57
  choosing, 57–58
  location of, 56
  plant pests, 57
  planting medium, 56

from Southeast Asia, 59–60
  watering, 57
  from Western
    Mediterranean, 61
Pneumonia, 49
Podarcis pityusensis, 63, 81
Poikilothermic animals, 7
Pothos, 59
Prey food, 29
Purchase, 24–25

Quarantine terrarium, 25–26

Rain forest plants, 58–60
Rain forest terrarium:
  epiphytes and
    branches, 20
  floor medium, 20
  walls, 19
  water containers, 20
Rats, 29, 33
Reflector lamps, 15
Rosemary, 61
Roundworms, 52

Salmonella, 51
Salt glands, 6
Sceloporus jarrovi, 53, 70
Sceloporus malachitus, 53,
  71
Sceloporus poinsetti, 53, 70
Screw pine, 61
Sedum, 60, 61
Sensory organs, 6
Sex determination, 41–42
Sickness:
  diagnosed by fecal exami-
    nation, 51–52, 55
  diagnosed with naked eye,
    46–51
Silk oak, 61
Skin, 7
Skin fungi, 49–50
Skin necrosis, 49

Skinks, 77–79
Small mammals, 28, 33
Snails, 27
Soa-soa, 76
Southern alligator lizard, *65,*
  82
Spathyphyllum, 58
Spiders, 28
Spiderwort, 59
Spiny lizard, *53,* 70
Spiny-tailed skink, *9,* 78
Spotlights, 17
Spurge, 60
Staghorn fern, 60, 61
Stephanotis, 60
Stress, 39
Striped Madagascar gecko, 67
Submissive behavior, 11
Sun terrarium, 13–14
Sword fern, 60
Syngonium, 58

Tail, 5–6
Tapeworms, 52
Tear glands, 6
Tegu, *54,* 80
Temperature control, 17–18
Terrarium, 9
  cleaning, 37
  covering, 13
  doors, 13
  heating, 15–16
  lighting, 16–17
  location, 12
  plants, 56–61
  shape, 12
  size, 12
  sun terrarium, 13–14
  temperature control, 17–18,
    36–37
  ventilation, 12–13
  See also Desert; Rain forest;
    Water terrarium
Terrestrial lizards, 5

Thermometer, 18
Ticks, 47
Tilqua gerrardii, 77
Tilqua gigas, 77–78
Timer, 17
Tokay gecko, *36,* 68
Tongue, 6
Transporting bag, 25
Tree-dwelling lizards, 5
Tropidurine lizard, *53,* 71
Tropidurus torquatus, 53, 71
True lizards, 80–81
Tupinambis teguixin
  nigropunctatus, 54, 80

Ultraviolet irridiation, 44
Ultraviolet lights, 17
Unisexual reproduction, 41

Vacation care, 40
Varanus exanthematicus, 54,
  83–84
Varanus niloticus, 54, 83
Ventilation, 12–13
Vermiculite, 43
Visceral gout, 52, 54
Vitamin A deficiency, 47
Vitamins, 28

Washington Agreement, 24,
  62
Water containers, 20, 21
Water-dwelling lizards, 5
Water filter, 18
Water terrarium, 22–23
Weeds, 29
Whiptails, 79–80
Wolf's milk, 60
Worms (food), 27
Worms (parasitic), 52

Perfect for Pet Owners!

PET OWNER'S MANUALS

Over 50 illustrations per book
(20 or more color photos),
72-80 pp., paperback.

AFRICAN GRAY PARROTS (3773-1)
AMAZON PARROTS (4035-X)
BANTAMS (3687-5)
BEAGLES (3829-0)
BEEKEEPING (4089-9)
BOXERS (4036-8)
CANARIES (4611-0)
CATS (4442-8)
CHINCHILLAS (4037-6)
CHOW-CHOWS (3952-1)
CICHLIDS (4597-1)
COCKATIELS (4610-2)
COCKATOOS (4159-3)
CONURES (4880-6)
DACHSHUNDS (2888-0)
DALMATIANS (4605-6)
DISCUS FISH (4669-2)
DOBERMAN PINSCHERS (2999-2)
DOGS (4822-9)
DWARF RABBITS (1352-2)
FEEDING AND SHELTERING
    BACKYARD BIRDS (4252-2)
FEEDING AND SHELTERING
    EUROPEAN BIRDS (2858-9)
FERRETS (2976-3)
GERBILS (3725-1)
GERMAN SHEPHERDS (2982-8)
GOLDEN RETRIEVERS (3793-6)
GOLDFISH (2975-5)
GOULDIAN FINCHES (4523-8)
GUINEA PIGS (4612-9)
HAMSTERS (4439-8)
IRISH SETTERS (4663-3)
KEESHONDEN (1560-6)
KILLIFISH (4475-4)
LABRADOR RETRIEVERS (3792-8)
LHASA APSOS (3950-5)
LIZARDS IN THE TERRARIUM (3925-4)
LONG-TAILED PARAKEETS (1351-4)
LORIES AND LORIKEETS (1567-3)
LOVEBIRDS (3726-X)
MACAWS (4768-0)
MICE (2921-6)
MINIATURE PIGS (1356-5)
MUTTS (4126-7)
MYNAHS (3688-3)
PARAKEETS (4437-1)
PARROTS (4823-7)
PERSIAN CATS (4405-3)
PIGEONS (4044-9)
POMERANIANS (4670-6)
PONIES (2856-2)
POODLES (2812-0)
RABBITS (4440-1)
RATS (4535-1)
ROTTWEILERS (4483-5)
SCHNAUZERS (3949-1)
SHAR-PEI (4834-2)
SHEEP (4091-0)
SHETLAND SHEEPDOGS (4264-6)
SHIH TZUS (4524-6)
SIAMESE CATS (4764-8)
SIBERIAN HUSKIES (4265-4)
SNAKES (2813-9)
SPANIELS (2424-9)
TROPICAL FISH (4700-1)
TURTLES (4702-8)
YORKSHIRE TERRIERS (4406-1)
ZEBRA FINCHES (3497-X)

NEW PET HANDBOOKS

Detailed, illustrated profiles (40-60
color photos), 144 pp., paperback.

NEW AQUARIUM FISH HANDBOOK
    (3682-4)
NEW AUSTRALIAN PARAKEET
    HANDBOOK (4739-7)
NEW BIRD HANDBOOK (4157-7)
NEW CANARY HANDBOOK (4879-2)
NEW CAT HANDBOOK (2922-4)
NEW COCKATIEL HANDBOOK (4201-8)
NEW DOG HANDBOOK (2857-0)
NEW DUCK HANDBOOK (4088-0)
NEW FINCH HANDBOOK (2859-7)
NEW GOAT HANDBOOK (4090-2)
NEW PARAKEET HANDBOOK (2985-2)
NEW PARROT HANDBOOK (3729-4)
NEW RABBIT HANDBOOK (4202-6)
NEW SALTWATER AQUARIUM
    HANDBOOK (4482-7)
NEW SOFTBILL HANDBOOK (4075-9)

NEW TERRIER HANDBOOK (3951-3)

REFERENCE BOOKS

Comprehensive, lavishly illustrated
references (60-300 color photos),
136-176 pp., hardcover & paperback
AQUARIUM FISH (1350-6)
AQUARIUM FISH BREEDING
    (4474-6)
AQUARIUM FISH SURVIVAL
    MANUAL (5686-8)
AQUARIUM PLANTS MANUAL
    (1687-4)
BEST PET NAME BOOK EVER, THE
    (4258-1)
CAT CARE MANUAL (5765-1),
CIVILIZING YOUR PUPPY (4953-5)
COMMUNICATING WITH YOUR
    DOG (4203-4)
COMPLETE BOOK OF
    BUDGERIGARS (6059-8),
COMPLETE BOOK OF CAT CARE,
    (4613-7)
COMPLETE BOOK OF DOG CARE,
    (4158-5)
COMPLETE BOOK OF PARROTS
    (5971-9)
DOG CARE MANUAL (5764-3)
FEEDING YOUR PET BIRD (1521-3)
GOLDFISH AND ORNAMENTAL
    CARP (5634-5)
GUIDE TO A WELL BEHAVED
    CAT (1476-6)
GUIDE TO HOME PET GROOMING
    (4298-0)
HOP TO IT: A Guide to
    Training Your Pet Rabbit
    (4551-3)
HORSE CARE MANUAL (5795-3)
HOW TO TALK TO YOUR
    CAT (1749-8)
HOW TO TEACH YOUR OLD DOG
    NEW TRICKS (4544-0),
LABYRINTH FISH (5635-3),
MACAWS (6073-3),
NONVENOMOUS SNAKES (5632-9),
WATER PLANTS IN THE AQUARIUM
    (3926-2), paperback

Barron's Educational Series, Inc. • 250 Wireless Blvd., Hauppauge, NY 11788
Call toll-free: 1-800-645-3476 • In Canada: Georgetown Book Warehouse
34 Armstrong Ave., Georgetown, Ont. L7G 4R9 • Call toll-free: 1-800-247-7160
ISBN prefix: 0-8120 • Order from your favorite book or pet store